Financial Accounting Principles
An Introductory Financial Accounting Course

Workbook

Neville Joffe

AME | Learning

ISBN: 978-1-926751-02-3

Financial Accounting Principles - Workbook
Author: Neville Joffe
Publisher: AME Learning
Developmental Editor: Trevor Monteiro
Production Editor: Diana Dragoman
Content Contributor: Penny Parker
Content Reviewer: Linda Zhang
Typesetter: Computer Composition of Canada
Project Coordinator: Linda Zhang
Cover Design: Anand Karat
Online Course Design & Production: AME Multimedia Team

Printed and bound in China

For more information contact:

AME Learning Inc.
303-1200 Sheppard Avenue East
Toronto, ON, Canada M2K 2S5
Phone: 416.848.4399
Toll-free: 1.888.401.3881
E-mail: info@amelearning.com
Visit our website at: www.amelearning.com

Table of Contents

Chapter 1

FINANCIAL STATEMENTS: PERSONAL ACCOUNTING

Assessment Questions

Question 1

Explain the role of the balance sheet. Why is it called a permanent record?

Question 2

Explain the role of the income statement. Why is it called a temporary record?

Question 3

What are assets?

Question 4

What are liabilities?

Question 5

How is net worth related to assets and liabilities?

Question 6

State the accounting equation.

Question 7

How does buying assets affect net worth?

Question 8

Which accounts are affected when reducing the principal portion of a debt? Are these accounts increased or decreased? How would this transaction impact net worth?

Question 9

How does paying interest on a loan affect net worth?

Question 10

Describe the relationship between net worth and cash.

Question 11

Define depreciation expense.

Question 12

What is the difference between accrual accounting and cash-based accounting? Provide an example.

Question 13

What is the matching principle? Why is it important?

Question 14

List three ways to recognize an expense.

Question 15

Why is the concept of materiality important for personal accounting purposes?

____

____

____

____

Question 16

When preparing a record of your personal finances, why is it important to separate normal revenues, such as your salary, from money received from lottery winnings or an inheritance?

____

____

____

____

Question 17

Explain the difference between book value and market value.

____

____

____

____

____

Application Questions

Question 1

Neil Rickett owns assets worth $400,000. Guy Boes owns assets worth $500,000. Neil owes $100,000. Guy owes $300,000. Who is wealthier? Why?

Question 2

On January 1, 2008 Kelly Peredo had cash of $7,000, other assets of $135,000 and liabilities of $105,500. On December 31, 2008 Kelly's cash amounted to $1,000 and other assets were in the amount of $152,000. The amount of liabilities remains the same. Was Kelly wealthier at the beginning of the year or at the end of the year? Explain your answer.

Question 3

Christian has cash of $50,000. His net worth is $35,000. Claire has a bank overdraft of $2,000 (i.e. owes the bank $2,000). Claire's net worth is $120,000. Who is wealthier? Why?

Question 4

In January, Eve Chevere earned a salary of $6,000. Her expenses were $3,600 and she paid off $1,000 of her credit card debt. Did her net worth increase or decrease in January? If so, by how much?

Question 5

Erik Abston has liabilities of $100,000 and a net worth of $200,000. Calculate the value of Erik's assets.

Question 6

Jessie Arnone has assets of $600,000 and a net worth of $400,000. How much does Jessie owe?

Question 7

Annabelle Oetting made a $1,000 payment to reduce her bank loan. Describe the effect of the payment on Annabelle's assets, liabilities, and net worth.

Question 8

Ted Nishida just lost his job. To raise some cash, Ted decided to sell the classic Ford Falcon car he bought a week ago. He managed to sell his classic car for $10,000, which is the exact same amount he paid for it. What effect did the sale have on Ted's cash, his total assets, and his net worth?

____

____

____

____

____

Question 9

Suzette purchased a laptop for $2,000. The laptop has a useful life of 5 years and will have no value after that. It depreciates in equal amounts throughout the 5 years of useful life.

a) By how much does Suzette's net worth change when she purchases the laptop?

____

____

____

b) How much is the depreciation amount per year? How would the amounts affect Suzette's net worth?

____

____

____

c) How much is the laptop worth (book value) at the beginning of the third year?

____

____

____

Question 10

Using the opening balances provided in the balance sheets below, enter the updated amounts for each transaction in the blank balance sheets marked "Answers".

1. Borrowed $4,000 from the bank.

Opening Balances

Assets		**Liabilities**	
Cash	5,000	Bank Loan	0
Value of Home	80,000	Credit Card Account	3,000
Automobile	20,000	Mortgage	50,000
Contents of Home	6,000	Automobile Loan	5,000
Investment	8,000	Student Loan	6,000
		Total Liabilities	64,000
		Net Worth	55,000
Total Assets	119,000	Liabilities + Net Worth	119,000

Answers

Assets		**Liabilities**	
Cash		Bank Loan	
Value of Home		Credit Card Account	
Automobile		Mortgage	
Contents of Home		Automobile Loan	
Investment		Student Loan	
		Total Liabilities	
		Net Worth	
Total Assets		Liabilities + Net Worth	

2. Sold Investments for $8,000 cash.

Opening Balances

Assets		**Liabilities**	
Cash	1,000	Bank Loan	0
Value of Home	80,000	Credit Card Account	3,000
Automobile	20,000	Mortgage	50,000
Contents of Home	6,000	Automobile Loan	5,000
Investment	8,000	Student Loan	6,000
		Total Liabilities	64,000
		Net Worth	51,000
Total Assets	115,000	Liabilities + Net Worth	115,000

Answers

Assets		**Liabilities**	
Cash		Bank Loan	
Value of Home		Credit Card Account	
Automobile		Mortgage	
Contents of Home		Automobile Loan	
Investment		Student Loan	
		Total Liabilities	
		Net Worth	
Total Assets		Liabilities + Net Worth	

3. Paid $1,000 to reduce an outstanding automobile loan (principal portion).

Opening Balances

Assets		**Liabilities**	
Cash	3,000	Bank Loan	0
Value of Home	80,000	Credit Card Account	3,000
Automobile	20,000	Mortgage	50,000
Contents of Home	6,000	Automobile Loan	5,000
		Student Loan	6,000
		Total Liabilities	64,000
		Net Worth	45,000
Total Assets	109,000	Liabilities + Net Worth	109,000

Answers

Assets		**Liabilities**	
Cash		Bank Loan	
Value of Home		Credit Card Account	
Automobile		Mortgage	
Contents of Home		Automobile Loan	
Investment		Student Loan	
		Total Liabilities	
		Net Worth	
Total Assets		Liabilities + Net Worth	

4. Bought a motorcycle for $6,000, paid a $1,000 deposit with cash and borrowed $5,000 from the bank.

Opening Balances

Assets		**Liabilities**	
Cash	2,000	Bank Loan	1,000
Value of Home	80,000	Credit Card Account	3,000
Automobile	20,000	Mortgage	50,000
Contents of Home	4,000	Automobile Loan	5,000
Motorcycle	-	Student Loan	6,000
		Total Liabilities	65,000
		Net Worth	41,000
Total Assets	106,000	Liabilities + Net Worth	106,000

Answers

Assets		**Liabilities**	
Cash		Bank Loan	
Value of Home		Credit Card Account	
Automobile		Mortgage	
Contents of Home		Automobile Loan	
Motorcycle		Student Loan	
		Total Liabilities	
		Net Worth	
Total Assets		Liabilities + Net Worth	

Question 11

Using the following chart, indicate whether there would be an increase, decrease or no change to the bank balance and net worth for the transactions provided. *The first transaction has been completed for you.*

		Bank Balance			Net Worth		
	Transaction	Increase	Decrease	No Change	Increase	Decrease	No Change
1	Deposit Salary	X			X		
2	Pay cash for food						
3	Borrow an automobile loan						
4	Sell a stereo for cash						
5	Pay student loan interest						
6	Reduce student loan principal						
7	Buy a new computer with cash						
8	Deposit a bank loan						
9	Pay entertainment expenses						
10	Record interest earned on savings						

Question 12

Using the following chart, indicate whether there would be an increase, decrease or no change to the bank balance and net worth for the transactions provided.

Update the new cash and net worth balances after each transaction.

			Bank Balance				Net Worth			
	Transaction	Amount	Increase	Decrease	No Change	Cash Balance	Increase	Decrease	No Change	Net Worth
	Opening Balance					1,000				3,000
1	Sell some personal assets for cash	3,000								
2	Borrow cash from a friend	1,000								
3	Pay cash for maintenance	500								
4	Record interest paid on car loan	200								
5	Pay back loan to a family member	1,000								
6	Reduce the principal potion of the car loan	300								
7	Lend a friend some cash	500								
8	Deposit a student loan	5,000								
9	A friend paid you back money borrowed	200								
10	Deposit salary from a summer job	3,000								

Question 13

On January 31, 2010 Darryl Pouliot decided that he wanted to track his finances. On this date, he had the following assets and liabilities:

• Automobile	25,000
• Automobile loan	7,000
• Bank loan	5,000
• Cash	5,000
• Contents of Home	10,000
• Credit card	3,000
• Mortgage on home	87,000
• Student loan	8,000
• Home	120,000

1. Calculate Darryl's net worth as at January 31st.

____

____

2. Prepare Darryl's balance sheet.

Darryl Poullot Balance Sheet As at January 31, 2010			
Assets		**Liabilities**	
		Total Liabilities	
		Net Worth	
Total Assets		Liabilities + Net Worth	

Question 14

The balance sheet for Chiavane Laprito as at May 31, 2010 is shown below:

Chiavane Laprito **Balance Sheet** **As at May 31, 2010**			
Assets		**Liabilities**	
Cash	$5,000	Credit Card	$2,000
Contents of Home	5,000	Automobile Loan	6,000
Automobile	12,000	Family Loan	5,000
Value of Home	150,000	Student Loan	6,000
		Mortgage on Home	130,000
		Total Liabilities	149,000
		Net Worth	23,000
Total Assets	$172,000	Liabilities + Net Worth	$172,000

In the month of June, Chiavane deposited her salary of $3,500 and paid expenses of $2,700 with cash. She also reduced the principal portion of her student loan by $500. Create her new balance sheet as at June 30, 2010.

Chiavane Laprito **Balance Sheet** **As at June 30, 2010**			
Assets		**Liabilities**	
		Total Liabilities	
		Net Worth	
Total Assets		Liabilities + Net Worth	

Question 15

State how the following transactions would impact net worth (increase, decrease, no change):

Item	Effect on Net Worth
Borrow Money	
Pay entertainment expense with cash	
Pay food expense with cash	
Buy assets with cash	
Charge home repairs expense on credit card	
Pay insurance expense with cash	
Pay loan principal with cash	
Purchase assets on account	
Receive salary	
Pay rent expense with cash	

Question 16

Sven Borg had the following assets and liabilities as at March 1, 2010:

	Assets	Liabilities
Cash	3,000	
Automobile	12,000	
Value of Home	130,000	
Contents of Home	4,000	
Mortgage		110,000
Student Loan		5,000
Credit Card		6,000
Home Depot Credit Card		2,000
Total	149,000	123,000

1. What is Sven's opening net worth on March 1st?

___

The following activities occurred in the month of March:

Received salary	$3,000
Charged food and gas to credit card	600
Paid cash for expenses	200
Charged repairs to credit card	400
Paid towards Home Depot debt	1,000
Recorded depreciation on automobile	500

2. What is Sven's closing net worth after recording the above transactions?

____

3. Prepare Sven's balance sheet as at March 31, 2010.

Sven Borg Balance Sheet As at March 31, 2010			
Assets		**Liabilities**	
		Total Liabilities	
		Net Worth	
Total Assets		Liabilities + Net Worth	

Question 17

As at July 31, 2010 Ted Merle owns the following: cash - $6,000, home - $200,000, automobile – $30,000, furniture - $10,000. Ted also owes the following: bank loan - $9,000, credit card amount - $5,000, mortgage – $90,000, automobile loan - $6,000, student loan - $20,000. Complete Ted's balance sheet and calculate his net worth.

Ted Merle Balance Sheet As at June 31, 2010			
Assets		**Liabilities**	
		Total Liabilities	
		Net Worth	
Total Assets		Liabilities + Net Worth	

Question 18

Using the balance sheet provided, calculate cash, total liabilities, net worth, and total liabilities plus net worth for John Smith as at January 31, 2010.

John Smith Balance Sheet As at January 31, 2010			
Assets		**Liabilities**	
Cash		Bank Loan	$5,000
Value of Home	110,000	Credit Card	10,000
Automobile	30,000	Mortgage on Home	80,000
Contents of Home	5,000	Automobile Loan	17,000
		Student Loan	3,000
		Total Liabilities	
		Net Worth	
Total Assets	$160,000	Liabilities + Net Worth	

Question 19

Complete the following chart by entering the number of the account affected (see list of accounts below) and whether that account would increase or decrease. Then determine whether the transaction would increase or decrease the bank balance and net worth. *The first transaction has been provided for you.*

#	Transaction	Account # - Increase or Decrease	Account # - Increase or Decrease	Bank Balance: Increase, Decrease or No Change	Net Worth: Increase, Decrease or No Change
	Buy a computer for cash	1 - Decrease	4 - Increase	Decrease	No Change
1	Receive a bill for expenses				
2	Pay a credit card bill				
3	Charge a new TV to a credit card				
4	Deposit salary check				
5	Receive interest on the savings account				
6	Pay cash for insurance				
7	Receive cash gifts for birthday celebration				
8	Buy a used car with cash				
9	Sell a stereo for cash				
10	Borrow cash from a friend				
11	Pay back the principal portion of a loan				

List of accounts:

Assets
1 Cash
2 Prepaid expenses
3 Automobile
4 Contents of home

Liabilities
5 Unpaid accounts
6 Credit card
7 Personal loan
8 Student loan
9 Automobile loan
10 Revenue
11 Expenses

Owner's Equity
12 Capital

Question 20

Complete this table by indicating the effect (increase, decrease, or no effect) on assets, liabilities, etc. *The first transaction has been provided for you.*

	Transaction	Assets	Liabilities	Revenue	Expenses	Net Worth
	Buy an asset using store credit	Increase	Increase	No Effect	No Effect	No Effect
a.	Charge expenses on credit card					
b.	Purchase food with cash					
c.	Pay credit card bill with cash					
d.	Pay loan principal					
e.	Record and pay loan interest					

Question 21

Record the name of the accounts being affected by each of the following transactions. Indicate whether the effect would be an increase or a decrease. In addition, state the impact of each transaction on bank balance and net worth. *The first transaction has been provided for you.*

	Transaction	Part 1: Account Name Inc or Dec	Part 2: Account Name Inc or Dec	Bank Balance: Inc, Dec or No Change	Net Worth: Inc, Dec or No Change
	Deposit salary	Cash - Inc	Revenue - Inc	Inc	Inc
1	Pay expenses with cash				
2	Charge a meal to a credit card				
3	Pay interest with cash				
4	Pay credit card bill				
5	Prepay rent for the next three months				
6	Borrow cash from the bank				
7	Win the lottery				
8	Recognize one month of prepaid rent as an expense				
9	Pay back student loan principal				
10	Borrow cash from a friend				

Question 22

For the transactions provided, mark with an "x" whether there would be an increase, decrease or no change to the bank balance and net worth.

		Bank Balance			Net Worth		
	Transaction	Increase	Decrease	No Change	Increase	Decrease	No Change
1	Deposit salary						
2	Buy food - charge to credit card						
3	Buy a used car - pay cash for the deposit						
4	Sell furniture for cash						
5	Pay student loan interest						
6	Reduce student loan principal						
7	Buy a new computer - use store credit						
8	Deposit a bank loan						
9	Prepay insurance for one year						
10	Record interest on savings account						
11	Receive a new TV as a gift						
12	Lend cash to a friend - to be paid back next month						
13	Depreciate the value of personal assets						
14	Recognize prepaid insurance for one month						
15	Prepaid insurance - receive refund for balance of the prepayment amount						

Question 23

Complete the T-Account worksheets on the opposite page for the following transactions and calculate net worth.

Opening balances:

Cash	1,000
Automobile	13,000
Computer (contents of home)	1,000
Credit card	5,000
Student loan	3,000
Automobile loan	5,000
Net worth	2,000

Transactions for the month of January:

1. Deposited salary	2,000
2. Paid cash for entertainment expenses	500
3. Paid interest on the student loan	100
4. Reduced the principal portion of the student loan	300
5. Paid interest on an overdue credit card balance	200
6. Paid interest on the automobile loan	300
7. Reduced the principal portion of the automobile loan	1,500
8. Paid telephone bill for the month with cash	100

BALANCE SHEET
As at January 31, 2010

ASSETS (what we OWN)

INCREASE (DR) DECREASE (CR)
- CASH +
Opening Balance:
Total:

INCREASE (DR) DECREASE (CR)
- VALUE OF HOME +
Opening Balance:
Total:

INCREASE (DR) DECREASE (CR)
- AUTOMOBILE +
Opening Balance:
Total:

INCREASE (DR) DECREASE (CR)
- CONTENTS OF HOME +
Opening Balance:
Total:

LIABILITIES (what we OWE)

DECREASE (DR) INCREASE (CR)
- CREDIT CARD +
Opening Balance:
Total:

DECREASE (DR) INCREASE (CR)
- STUDENT LOAN +
Opening Balance:
Total:

DECREASE (DR) INCREASE (CR)
- AUTOMOBILE LOAN +
Opening Balance:
Total:

NET WORTH

Opening Net Worth (Same as closing from previous period)	
PLUS Surplus (Deficit) (from Income Stmt)	+
Equals Closing Net Worth	=

TOTAL ASSETS $__________

= TOTAL LIABILITIES __________
+ OWNER'S EQUITY __________ } $__________

INCOME STATEMENT
For the month ending January 31, 2010

REVENUE (WAGES & INTEREST)

DECREASE (DR) - INCREASE (CR) +

MINUS
EXPENSES

INCREASE (DR) DECREASE (CR)
+ CLOTHING -

INCREASE (DR) DECREASE (CR)
+ ENTERTAINMENT -

INCREASE (DR) DECREASE (CR)
+ FOOD -

INCREASE (DR) DECREASE (CR)
+ INTEREST -

INCREASE (DR) DECREASE (CR)
+ RENT -

INCREASE (DR) DECREASE (CR)
+ TELEPHONE -

TOTAL REVENUE $__________

- EXPENSES __________

= SURPLUS (DEFICIT) $__________

Question 24

Complete the T-Account worksheets on the opposite page for the following transactions and calculate net worth.

Opening balances:

Daily banking account	2,000
Contents of home	5,000
Student loan	4,000
Net worth	3,000

Transactions for the month of January:

1.	Paid cash to purchase a new stereo (contents of home)	500
2.	Deposited salary	2,500
3.	Received interest on daily banking account	100
4.	Transferred funds from the daily banking account to the savings account because of higher interest rate	600
5.	Sold an old stereo for cash	100
6.	Paid the principal portion of the student loan	300
7.	Paid interest on the student loan	700
8.	Paid other miscellaneous living expenses	1,000
9.	Bought furniture on credit	400

Note: we assume all assets are sold at the same value as recorded on the balance sheet. The difference between the book value (the value recorded on the balance sheet) and market value will be taught in the forthcoming chapters.

BALANCE SHEET
As at January 31, 2010

ASSETS (what we OWN)

INCREASE (DR) DECREASE (CR)

- DAILY BANKING +

Opening Balance:

Total:

INCREASE (DR) DECREASE (CR)

- SAVINGS ACCOUNT +

Opening Balance:

Total:

INCREASE (DR) DECREASE (CR)

- AUTOMOBILE +

Total:

INCREASE (DR) DECREASE (CR)

- CONTENTS OF HOME +

Opening Balance:

Total:

LIABILITIES (what we OWE)

DECREASE (DR) INCREASE (CR)

- CREDIT CARD +

Total:

DECREASE (DR) INCREASE (CR)

- STUDENT LOAN +

Opening Balance:

Total:

DECREASE (DR) INCREASE (CR)

- AUTOMOBILE LOAN +

Total:

NET WORTH

Opening Net Worth (Same as closing from previous period)	
PLUS Surplus (Deficit) (from Income Stmt)	+
Equals Closing Net Worth	=

TOTAL ASSETS $__________

= TOTAL LIABILITIES __________
+ OWNER'S EQUITY __________ } $__________

INCOME STATEMENT
For the month ending January 31, 2010

REVENUE (WAGES & INTEREST)

DECREASE (DR) - INCREASE (CR) +

MINUS
EXPENSES

INCREASE (DR) DECREASE (CR)

+ ENTERTAINMENT -

INCREASE (DR) DECREASE (CR)

+ FOOD -

INCREASE (DR) DECREASE (CR)

+ INTEREST -

INCREASE (DR) DECREASE (CR)

+ MICSCELLANEOUS -

INCREASE (DR) DECREASE (CR)

+ RENT -

INCREASE (DR) DECREASE (CR)

+ TELEPHONE -

TOTAL REVENUE $__________

- EXPENSES __________

= SURPLUS (DEFICIT) $__________

Question 25

Complete the T-Account worksheets on the opposite page for the following transactions and calculate net worth.

Opening balances:

Cash	1,000
Contents of home	4,000
Credit card	1,000
Student loan	2,000
Net worth	2,000

Transactions for the month of February:

1.	Deposited salary	2,000
2.	Bought a new TV - charged to credit card	600
3.	Prepaid the car insurance for one year	600
4.	Recognized one month of prepaid insurance as an expense	50
5.	Bought a show ticket - charged to credit card	50
6.	Sold some old furniture for cash	200
7.	Paid interest on the overdue credit card debt	100
8.	Reduced the amount owing on credit card	400
9.	Sold some personal assets (contents of home)	800
10.	Deposited cash gifts	5,000

BALANCE SHEET
As at February 28, 2010

ASSETS (what we OWN)

INCREASE (DR) DECREASE (CR)

- CASH +

Opening Balance:

Total:

INCREASE (DR) DECREASE (CR)

- PREPAID EXPENSES +

Total:

INCREASE (DR) DECREASE (CR)

- AUTOMOBILE +

Opening Balance:

Total:

INCREASE (DR) DECREASE (CR)

+ CONTENTS OF HOME -

Opening Balance:

Total:

LIABILITIES (what we OWE)

DECREASE (DR) INCREASE (CR)

- CREDIT CARD +

Opening Balance:

Total:

DECREASE (DR) INCREASE (CR)

- STUDENT LOAN +

Opening Balance:

Total:

NET WORTH

Opening Net Worth (Same as closing from previous period)	
PLUS Capital	+
PLUS Surplus (Deficit) (from Income Stmt)	+
Equals Closing Net Worth	=

TOTAL ASSETS $__________

= TOTAL LIABILITIES __________

+ OWNER'S EQUITY __________ } $__________

INCOME STATEMENT
For the month ending February 28, 2010

REVENUE (WAGES & INTEREST)

DECREASE (DR) - INCREASE (CR) +

MINUS

EXPENSES

INCREASE (DR) DECREASE (CR)

+ DEPRECIATION -

INCREASE (DR) DECREASE (CR)

+ ENTERTAINMENT -

INCREASE (DR) DECREASE (CR)

+ INSURANCE -

INCREASE (DR) DECREASE (CR)

+ INTEREST -

INCREASE (DR) DECREASE (CR)

+ RENT -

INCREASE (DR) DECREASE (CR)

+ TELEPHONE -

TOTAL REVENUE $__________

- EXPENSES __________

= SURPLUS (DEFICIT) $__________

Question 26

Complete the T-Account worksheets on the opposite page for the following transactions and calculate net worth.

Opening balances:

Cash	11,000
Contents of home	5,000
Automobile	12,000
Credit card	2,000
Automobile loan	7,000
Student loan	5,000
Net worth	14,000

Transactions for the month of February:

1.	Recorded deposit of extra money earned from babysitting	300
2.	Paid cash for food	20
3.	Reduced student loan principal	500
4.	Purchased a new TV using cash	300
5.	Paid cash for interest owing on auto loan	200
6.	Sold some old furniture for cash (contents of home)	600
7.	Deposited salary	2,000
8.	Prepaid insurance for one year	2,400
9.	Paid for car maintenance - charged to credit card	150
10.	Recognized prepaid insurance for one month	200

BALANCE SHEET
As at February 28, 2010

ASSETS (what we OWN)

INCREASE (DR) DECREASE (CR)
- CASH +

Opening Balance:

Total:

INCREASE (DR) DECREASE (CR)
- PREPAID EPENSES +

Total:

INCREASE (DR) DECREASE (CR)
- AUTOMOBILE +

Opening Balance:

Total:

INCREASE (DR) DECREASE (CR)
- CONTENTS OF HOME +

Opening Balance:

Total:

LIABILITIES (what we OWE)

DECREASE (DR) INCREASE (CR)
- CREDIT CARD +

Opening Balance:

Total:

DECREASE (DR) INCREASE (CR)
- STUDENT LOAN +

Opening Balance:

Total:

DECREASE (DR) INCREASE (CR)
- AUTOMOBILE LOAN +

Opening Balance:

Total:

NET WORTH

Opening Net Worth (Same as closing from previous period)	
PLUS Surplus (Deficit) (from Income Stmt)	+
Equals Closing Net Worth	=

TOTAL ASSETS $________

= TOTAL LIABILITIES ________
+ OWNER'S EQUITY ________ } $________

INCOME STATEMENT
For the month ending February 28, 2010

REVENUE (WAGES & INTEREST)

DECREASE (DR) - INCREASE (CR) +

MINUS
EXPENSES

INCREASE (DR) DECREASE (CR)
+ DEPRECIATION -

INCREASE (DR) DECREASE (CR)
+ FOOD -

INCREASE (DR) DECREASE (CR)
+ INSURANCE -

INCREASE (DR) DECREASE (CR)
+ INTEREST -

INCREASE (DR) DECREASE (CR)
+ MAINTENANCE -

INCREASE (DR) DECREASE (CR)
+ RENT -

TOTAL REVENUE $________

- EXPENSES ________

= SURPLUS (DEFICIT) $________

Question 27

Complete the following accrual exercise by recording each entry for the transactions listed using the balance sheet worksheet provided on the opposite page.

Once you have recorded all the entries, complete the balance sheet by adding up assets, liabilities and net worth.

Transactions for the month of February:

1.	Deposited salary (this transaction has been done for you)	2,000
2.	Paid cash for entertainment	300
3.	Reduced car loan (principal portion)	1,000
4.	Deposited wages from a part-time job	1,000
5.	Bought clothing - charged to credit card	100
6.	Paid cash for interest on car loan	200
7.	Bought a TV - charged to credit card	500
8.	Paid for maintenance - charged to credit card	400

Important!

Once you have completed the exercise, review the balance sheet with this in mind: *what caused the changes to net worth?*

Balance Sheet
As at February 28, 2010

ASSETS

CASH

Opening: $ 0

Closing: $

CONTENTS OF HOME

Opening: $ 3,000

Closing: $

CAR

Opening: $ 6,000

Closing: $

TOTAL ASSETS $

LIABILITIES

UNPAID ACCOUNTS

Opening: $ 0

Closing: $

CAR LOAN

Opening: $ 3,000

Closing: $

TOTAL LIABILITIES $ 3,000

NET WORTH

Opening: $ 6,000

New Balance ______________

New Balance ______________

New Balance ______________

New Balance ______________

New Balance ______________

New Balance ______________

LIABILITIES + NET WORTH $

Question 28

Complete each entry for the same transactions as in Question 27 using the balance sheet and income statement worksheets provided on the opposite page.

Once all transactions have been entered, subtract the total expenses from total revenue to determine the amount of surplus or deficit. Update the net worth by transferring the surplus (or deficit) from the income statement to the balance sheet.

Transactions:

1.	Deposited salary	2,000
2.	Paid cash for entertainment	300
3.	Reduced car loan (principal portion)	1,000
4.	Deposited wages from a part-time job	1,000
5.	Bought clothing - charged to credit card	100
6.	Paid cash for interest on car loan	200
7.	Bought a TV - charged to credit card	500
8.	Paid for maintenance - charged to credit card	400

Important!

Review the balance sheet and the table you completed with regards to the changes in net worth. Now you know what caused these changes in net worth.

BALANCE SHEET
As at February 28, 2010

ASSETS		LIABILITIES	
CASH		**UNPAID ACCOUNTS**	
Opening:	$ 0	Opening:	$ 0
Closing:	$	Closing:	$
CONTENTS OF HOME		**CAR LOAN**	
Opening:	$ 3,000	Opening:	$ 3,000
Closing:	$	Closing:	$
CAR		TOTAL LIABILITIES	$
Opening:	$ 6,000	**NET WORTH**	
Closing:	$	Opening Net Worth:	$ 6,000
		+	
		Surplus:	$
		=	
		Closing Net Worth:	$
TOTAL ASSETS	$	LIABILITIES + NET WORTH	$

INCOME STATEMENT
As at February 28, 2010

REVENUE

Total: $

EXPENSES

Total: $

Revenue:	$
-	
Expenses:	$
=	
Surplus (Deficit):	$

Critical Thinking:

You are a college student who rents an apartment, owns a car and works hard to help put yourself through school. Since you acknowledge the importance of budgeting, you maintain accurate financial records of all your monthly activities. Record all the financial transactions that occur this month. First enter the opening balances on your balance sheet followed by this month's activity.

Explain, in detail, why the change to the cash balance and the change to net worth are so different.

Chapter 2

LINKING PERSONAL ACCOUNTING TO BUSINESS ACCOUNTING

Assessment Questions

Question 1

Describe the sequence of assets and liabilities on a balance sheet.

Question 2

Give the formula for ending capital balance.

Question 3

From a legal perspective, is a sole proprietorship separate from its owner? Describe the risks to the sole proprietor if the business is unable to pay its debts.

Application Questions

Question 1

Jonathan MacGregor decided to operate a lawn mowing business, called City's Lawnmower, during the summer months. Record the following transactions for Jonathan's business on the T-Accounts on the opposite page, and then complete the income statement and balance sheet. You are required to fill in the account names for each T-Account.

Transactions for the month of March:

1.	Owner deposited cash into the business in the form of owner's equity	$5,000
2.	Purchased a lawnmower from large retailer - to be paid next month	600
3.	Purchased other equipment such as rakes, trimmers, etc. - to be paid next month	700
4.	The bank agreed to loan Jonathan $6,000 - the principal amount is to be paid back within 12 months at $500 per month - the interest will cost $50 per month	6,000
5.	Insurance had to be purchased to cover any potential damages to property, and for Jonathan's truck and equipment - he had no credit history so the insurance company requested a prepayment of insurance for twelve months	1,200
6.	Recorded cash sales for the first month	4,000
7.	Paid miscellaneous expenses with cash	300
8.	Paid a part-time employee	600
9.	Recorded cash payment for maintenance	400
10.	Recognized the first month of prepaid insurance as an expense	100
11.	Paid outstanding accounts payable	1,000
12.	Paid bank loan principal	500
13.	Paid interest owing on bank loan	50
14.	Recorded depreciation of long-term assets	100
15.	Withdrew money, at the end of the month, for personal use	2,000

BALANCE SHEET
As at March 31, 2010

ASSETS (what we OWN)

INCREASE (DR) DECREASE (CR)

+ CASH -

Opening Balance:

Total:

INCREASE (DR) DECREASE (CR)

+ PREPAID EXPENSES -

Opening Balance:

Total:

INCREASE (DR) DECREASE (CR)

+ LONG-TERM ASSETS -

Opening Balance:

Total:

LIABILITIES (what we OWE)

DECREASE (DR) INCREASE (CR)

- ACCOUNTS PAYABLE +

Total:

DECREASE (DR) INCREASE (CR)

- BANK LOAN +

Total:

OWNER'S EQUITY

Opening Capital Balance		
PLUS Additional Capital		+
PLUS Net Income (Loss)		+
MINUS Owner's Withdrawals		-
EQUALS Closing Capital Balance		=

TOTAL ASSETS $______

= TOTAL LIABILITIES ______

+ OWNER'S EQUITY ______ } $______

INCOME STATEMENT
For the month ending March 31, 2010

REVENUE

DECREASE (DR) - INCREASE (CR) +

MINUS

EXPENSES

INCREASE (DR) DECREASE (CR)

+ ADVERTISING -

INCREASE (DR) DECREASE (CR)

+ DEPRECIATION -

INCREASE (DR) DECREASE (CR)

+ INSURANCE -

INCREASE (DR) DECREASE (CR)

+ INTEREST -

INCREASE (DR) DECREASE (CR)

+ MAINTENANCE -

INCREASE (DR) DECREASE (CR)

+ MISCELLANEOUS -

INCREASE (DR) DECREASE (CR)

+ SALARIES -

INCREASE (DR) DECREASE (CR)

+ TELEPHONE -

TOTAL REVENUE $______

- EXPENSES ______

= PROFIT (LOSS) $______

Complete the income statement and balance sheet for this exercise.

City's Lawnmower Income Statement For the month ending March 31, 2010	
Revenue	
Total Revenue	
Expenses	
Total Expenses	
Net Income (Loss)	

City's Lawnmower Balance Sheet As at March 31, 2010			
Assets		**Liabilities**	
		Total Liabilities	
		Owner's Equity	
Total Assets		**Total Liabilities & Owner's Equity**	

Question 2

World's Computer Service Centre has hired you to update their transactions for the month of June. Record the following transactions on the T-Account worksheets on the opposite page and then complete the income statement and balance sheet. You are required to fill in the account names for each T-Account.

World's Computer Service Centre Balance Sheet As at May 31, 2010			
Assets		**Liabilities**	
Cash	25,000	Accounts Payable	9,500
Prepaid Expenses	2,400	Bank Loan	12,000
Long-Term Assets	60,000	Total Liabilities	21,500
		Owner's Equity	65,900
Total Assets	**87,400**	**Total Liabilities & Owner's Equity**	**87,400**

During June, the business engaged in the following transactions:

1. Borrowed money from the bank	$90,000
2. Paid cash to a real estate company to acquire land	80,000
3. Performed service for a customer and received cash	3,000
4. Recorded maintenance expense on account	600
5. Provided services to a customer and earned cash	4,200
6. Paid cash to reduce the balance of accounts payable	1,500
7. Received telephone bill that will be paid next month	150
8. Paid employee salary	2,000
9. Recognized one month of prepaid insurance as an expense	200
10. Paid rent with cash	2,500

BALANCE SHEET
As at June 30, 2010

ASSETS (what we OWN)

INCREASE (DR) DECREASE (CR)
+ CASH -
Opening Balance:
Total:

INCREASE (DR) DECREASE (CR)
+ PREPAID EXPENSES -
Opening Balance:
Total:

INCREASE (DR) DECREASE (CR)
+ LONG-TERM ASSETS -
Opening Balance:
Total:

LIABILITIES (what we OWE)

DECREASE (DR) INCREASE (CR)
- ACCOUNTS PAYABLE +
Opening Balance:
Total:

DECREASE (DR) INCREASE (CR)
- BANK LOAN +
Opening Balance:
Total:

OWNER'S EQUITY

Opening Capital Balance		
		+
PLUS Additional Capital		
		+
PLUS Net Income (Loss)		
		-
MINUS Owner's Withdrawals		
		=
EQUALS Closing Capital Balance		

TOTAL ASSETS $__________

= TOTAL LIABILITIES __________
+ OWNER'S EQUITY __________ } $__________

INCOME STATEMENT
For the month ending June 30, 2010

REVENUE

DECREASE (DR) - INCREASE (CR) +

MINUS
EXPENSES

INCREASE (DR) DECREASE (CR)
+ DEPRECIATION -

INCREASE (DR) DECREASE (CR)
+ INSURANCE -

INCREASE (DR) DECREASE (CR)
+ INTEREST -

INCREASE (DR) DECREASE (CR)
+ RENT -

INCREASE (DR) DECREASE (CR)
+ MAINTENANCE -

INCREASE (DR) DECREASE (CR)
+ SALARIES -

INCREASE (DR) DECREASE (CR)
+ TELEPHONE -

TOTAL REVENUE $__________
- EXPENSES __________
= PROFIT (LOSS) $__________

Complete the income statement and balance sheet for Question 2.

World's Computer Service Centre Income Statement For the month ending June 30, 2010	
Revenue	
Total Revenue	
Expenses	
Total Expenses	
Net Income (Loss)	

World's Computer Service Centre Balance Sheet As at June 30, 2010			
Assets		**Liabilities**	
		Total Liabilities	
		Owner's Equity	
Total Assets		**Total Liabilities & Owner's Equity**	

Question 3

Belinda was confused as to why there was such a difference between the net income earned and the change to cash. Complete this exercise to indicate how each transaction impacts (increases, decreases, does not change) the cash and equity balances of the company. *The first question is completed as an example.*

		Amount	Cash Balance	Equity Balance
	Owner's Investment	$20,000	Increase	Increase
1	Bank loan	12,000		
2	Cash purchase of furniture and computers	15,000		
3	Prepayment of "errors & omissions" insurance	1,200		
4	Cash sales for the month	15,000		
5	Cash payment for assistant's payroll	3,000		
6	Cash payment for monthly rent	1,000		
7	Advertisement in magazine to be paid next month	2,000		
8	Cash payment for various travel expenses	1,500		
9	Plumbing expense to be paid next month	50		
10	Interest payment on bank loan	300		
11	Payment to reduce bank loan principal	250		
12	Depreciation of long-term assets	150		
13	Payment to reduce the balance of accounts payable	5,000		
14	Withdrawal made by owner for personal use	3,000		

Chapter 3

ACCOUNTING PRINCIPLES AND PRACTICES IN A BUSINESS

Question 1

1. Assume that you have the desire and qualifications to enter any one of the professional accounting designation programs. Discuss how you would decide which program to choose.

2. During your accounting studies, you may be exposed to different fields of accounting. Discuss the characteristics of each field. State which field is the most interesting to you and provide reasons.

3. List the three major types of business models, and give three examples of each.

4. Name and describe the two major classes of stakeholders in a business.

5. If you were to open a restaurant business, list three GAAP rules that may relate to your business, and the importance of each rule.

6. List five items that may be included in a code of ethics developed by a professional accounting body.

7. How might an accountant decide whether or not a particular action is ethical?

Question 2

1. What are the benefits of a good accounting system?

2. Discuss why GAAP is important for a company's accountants, employees, and investors.

3. What is a proprietorship?

4. What is a partnership?

5. What does it mean if a partner is subject to unlimited liability? Why would a limited liability partnership sometimes be preferred?

6. What is a co-operative organization?

7. What kind of organizations are classified as non-profit?

8. What is a corporation? What is the main difference between a corporation and a proprietorship?

9. If you have the opportunity to start your own business, what kind of products or services would you provide? Which type of business organization would you choose to form and why?

Notes

Chapter 4

BUSINESS ACCOUNTING CYCLE

Assessment Questions

Question 1

To familiarize yourself with debit and credit transactions, complete this exercise using the transactions below. Record the account for each pair of transactions and note whether the result is a debit or credit to that account. Also note whether the result is an increase or decrease.

Transactions:

1.	Cash sales *(completed for you as an example)*	$6,300
2.	Charge entertainment expenses to a credit card	2,500
3.	Pay cash for building maintenance	1,000
4.	Buy a computer - to be paid next month	1,500
5.	Pay staff salaries	2,000
6.	Pay back a portion of bank loan (principal only)	1,000
7.	Depreciate equipment	500
8.	Pay the interest portion of bank loan	100
9.	Pay cash for monthly rent expenses	2,200
10.	Pay cash for telephone expenses	150
11.	Receive interest on savings account	80
12.	Pay cash for car insurance used this period	500
13.	Sell furniture for cash at the value listed on the balance sheet	800
14.	Charge a newspaper advertisement to a credit card	450
15.	Receive lawyer's invoice for services rendered	950
16.	Pay cash for miscellaneous living expenses	400
17.	Pay accounts payable	1,300

	Account Name	Increase or Decrease	DR	CR
1	Cash	Increase	$6,300	
	Revenue	Increase		$6,300

Question 2

Convert the following journal entries into t-account entries using the blank worksheet on the opposite page. *We have provided an example.*

Example		DR	CR
	Cash	2,000	
	Revenue		2,000
	Deposit cash sale		

1.		DR	CR
	Accounts Payable	1,500	
	Cash		1,500
	Pay outstanding credit bill		

2.		DR	CR
	Depreciation Expense	300	
	Long-term Assets		300
	Record depreciation of long-term assets		

3.		DR	CR
	Miscellaneous Expenses	200	
	Cash		200
	Pay miscellaneous cash expenses		

4.		DR	CR
	Maintenance Expense	3,500	
	Accounts Payable		3,500
	Record maintenance expense on account		

5.		DR	CR
	Insurance Expense	500	
	Prepaid Expenses		500
	Recognize insurance expense for one month		

6.		DR	CR
	Cash	800	
	Long-term Assets		800
	Sell long-term assets for cash		

7.		DR	CR
	Bank Loan	5,000	
	Cash		5,000
	Pay principal portion of bank loan		

8.		DR	CR
	Prepaid Expenses	2,400	
	Cash		2,400
	Prepay insurance for one year		

Example

Cash	
DR	**CR**
2,000	

Revenue	
DR	**CR**
	2,000

1.

2.

3.

4.

5.

6.

7.

8.

Question 3

1. Explain the role of the journal.

2. Explain the role of the general ledger.

3. Explain the role of the trial balance.

4. Explain the role of the post-closing trial balance.

5. Explain the role of the statement of owner's equity.

Question 4

1. Describe the six steps for completing the accounting cycle.

2. What is the purpose of closing the books?

____

____

____

____

____

3. The debit and credit reference guide in this chapter is shown below (with account categories removed). Fill in the account categories (assets, liabilities, revenue, expenses, owner's equity) based on the debits and credits provided.

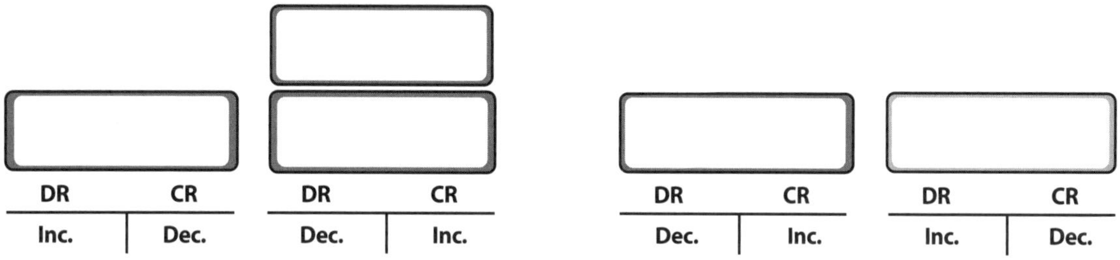

4. What is the chart of accounts? Discuss the importance of the chart of accounts.

____

____

____

____

____

5. Complete the following trial balance worksheet:

TRIAL BALANCE - WORKSHEET - FOR THE PERIOD ENDING JANUARY 31, 2010						
	TRIAL BALANCE		INCOME STATEMENT		BALANCE SHEET	
ACCOUNT TITLES	**DR**	**CR**	**DR**	**CR**	**DR**	**CR**
Cash	2,700					
Long-Term Assets	5,000					
Accounts Payable		900				
Revenue		9,000				
Rent	1,000					
Salaries and Bonuses	1,200					
Totals						
NET INCOME (LOSS)						
Allocated Net Income (loss) to Balance Sheet						
TOTAL						

6. Explain the use of the income summary account.

____

____

____

Question 5

Prepare the debit and credit transactions based on the descriptions provided. Indicate whether equity would increase, decrease, or stay the same after each transaction.

1.	DESCRIPTION	DR	CR
	Deposit $20,000 bank loan		

Equity:

2.	DESCRIPTION	DR	CR
	Deposit cash sales of $5,000		

Equity:

3.	DESCRIPTION	DR	CR
	Pay accounts payable of $8,000		

Equity:

4.	DESCRIPTION	DR	CR
	Prepay insurance of $2,000		

Equity:

5.	DESCRIPTION	DR	CR
	Record depreciation of $500		

Equity:

6.	DESCRIPTION	DR	CR
	Recognize $100 in prepaid insurance		

Equity:

Question 6

1. A list of accounts is shown below. Identify the normal balance of each account (debit or credit).

Accounts Payable	
Bank Loan	
Salaries Expense	
Capital Account	
Cash	
Interest Earned on Savings	
Revenue	
Owner's Equity	

2. On July 6, 2010, a company recognized $300 of prepaid insurance as an expense. Prepare the journal entry to record the transaction.

DATE	DESCRIPTION	DR	CR

3. A company wants to add the following accounts to its chart of accounts. Using the account framework discussed in this chapter, assign account numbers to the accounts.

Name	Account Numbers
Cash (bank account)	
Cable Expense	
Accounts Payable	
Depreciation Expense	
Long-Term Assets – Equipment	
Interest Earned on Note Receivable	
Prepaid Insurance	
Revenue	

4. The following balances are shown in the general ledger:

   Revenues = $10,000

   Expenses: Maintenance = $200, Rent = $1,500, Telephone = $500, Salaries = $2,800

Record the entries to close the books for the year. Assume the company uses the "income summary" method.

DATE	DESCRIPTION	DR	CR

5. Use the information on the trial balance worksheet to prepare a post-closing trial balance.

COMPANY XYZ – TRIAL BALANCE – WORKSHEET – FOR THE MONTH ENDING JUNE 30, 2010						
	TRIAL BALANCE		INCOME STATEMENT		BALANCE SHEET	
ACCOUNT TITLES	**DR**	**CR**	**DR**	**CR**	**DR**	**CR**
Cash	600				600	
Long-Term Assets	900				900	
Accounts Payable		500				500
Repair Revenue		2,000		2,000		
Rent	400		400			
Salaries and Bonuses	600		600			
Totals	2,500	2,500	1,000	2,000	1,500	500
NET INCOME (LOSS)			1,000			
Allocated Net Income (Loss) to Balance Sheet						1,000
TOTAL	2,500	2,500	2,000	2,000	1,500	1,500

Company XYZ Post-Closing Trial Balance For the Month Ending June 30, 2010		
	DR	**CR**

6. A company is preparing its year-end financial statements. The following adjustments are required:

- Depreciation for the year - $10,000
- $1,000 of prepaid insurance should be recognized as an expense
- The bank statement shows $200 of interest earned and the amount has not been recorded in the books

Prepare the required journal entries.

DATE	DESCRIPTION	DR	CR

7. The accountant has prepared a trial balance, but is having difficulty getting it to balance. Use the knowledge of normal debit and credit balances to help the accountant balance the trial balance. Also, arrange the trial balance in the usual order of accounts. Assume all accounts have normal balances.

Trial Balance - Worksheet		
	DR	CR
Accounts Payable	2,000	
Advertising	6,800	
Depreciation Expense		3,280
Bad Debts	500	
Cash	6,600	
Current Bank Loan		20,000
Equipment Loan		5,000
Furniture and Fixtures	150,000	
Insurance	1,400	
Inventory	30,000	
Long-Term Bank Loan		50,000
Maintenance	4,900	
Owner's Capital		90,000
Other Expenses	51,866	
Prepaid Expenses	1,000	
Sales Revenue		88,746
TOTALS	254,466	257,026

Trial Balance - Worksheet		
	DR	CR

Question 7

On the chart below, check the appropriate chart of accounts category to indicate where the various accounts belong.

Account	Assets	Liabilities	Revenue	Expenses	Equity
Sales					
Automobile					
Cash					
Computer					
Utility					
Insurance					
Bank Loan					
Owner's Drawings					
Prepaid Expenses					
Accounts Receivable					
Depreciation					
Interest Paid					
Salaries and Bonuses					
Equipment					
Accounts Payable					
Capital Account					

Question 8

Enter the correct debit and credit entries in the table provided below. *The first entry has been completed for you.*

Transaction	DR	CR
Deposit cash sales	***Cash***	***Sales***
Pay for rent with cash		
Record professional service fees to be paid next month		
Pay cash towards accounts payable		
Deposit owner's capital		
Record depreciation		
Buy assets with a loan		
Borrow money from the bank		
Pay interest with cash		
Record interest received from investments		
Pay bank loan principal		
Prepaid rent for the next three months		
Recognize one month of prepaid insurance as an expense		

Question 9

Using the chart below, identify whether the general ledger accounts should have a debit or credit balance in the normal course of business.

Account	DR or CR Balance
Accounts Payable	
Advertising Expense	
Depreciation Expense	
Bank Charges	
Bank Loan	
Cash	
Revenue	
Credit Card Bill	
Long-Term Assets	
Legal Fees	
Mortgage	
Accounts Receivable	
Prepaid Expenses	
Rent Expense	
Repairs and Maintenance Expense	
Salary Expense	
Telephone Expense	
Interest Expense	

Application Questions

Question 1

1. Prepare the closing entries at the end of the accounting period using the financial statements provided (assume the company closes the accounts directly to owner's capital).

A-Z Company Ltd.
Income Statement
For Month Ending December 31, 2010

Revenue	$140,000
Expenses	
Advertising	$ 6,000
Depreciation	16,400
Insurance	3,600
Maintenance	7,000
Rent	24,000
Salary	60,000
Utility	3,000
Total Expenses	$120,000
Net Income (Loss)	???

A-Z Company Ltd.
Balance Sheet
As at December 31, 2010

ASSETS	
Current Assets	
Cash	$ 4,000
Accounts Receivable	12,000
Prepaid Expenses	1,000
Inventory	30,000
Total Current Assets	**47,000**
Long-Term Assets	
Furniture & Fixtures	150,000
Total Assets	**$197,000**
LIABILITIES	
Current Liabilities	
Accounts Payable	$ 2,000
Unearned Revenue	10,000
Current Bank Loan	20,000
Equipment Loan	5,000
Total Current Liabilities	**37,000**
Long-Term Liabilities	
Bank Loan	50,000
Total Liabilities	**$ 87,000**
OWNER'S EQUITY	
Opening Capital	$ 90,000
Net Income (Loss)	???
Closing Capital	???
Liabilities + Equity	**$197,000**

DATE	DESCRIPTION	DR	CR

2. By what amount will the owner's capital account change?

___

3. Will there be a debit or a credit to the owner's capital account?

___

Question 2

The opening balances, chart of accounts and a list of transactions from Denvic repairs inc. are shown below. Prepare the general journal entries to record these transactions, post them to the general ledger, and complete the trial balance worksheet. In addition, create the income statement, balance sheet and statement of owner's equity.

Opening balances:

Cash	$50,000
Accounts Receivable	1,000
Prepaid Expenses	6,000
Equipment	5,000
Accounts Payable	20,000
Owner's Equity	42,000

The transactions for the month of June:

Jun 2	Received and deposited payment from repair work	$2,000
Jun 3	Paid employee salary	600
Jun 4	Paid rent with cash	400
Jun 5	Purchased equipment to be paid next month	9,000
Jun 6	Paid cash towards accounts payable	400

Use the following chart of accounts:

Account Description	Account #
ASSETS - Category 1	
Cash	101
Accounts Receivable	105
Prepaid Expenses	110
Inventory	115
Fixed Assets - Equipment	120
Accumulated Depreciation	130
LIABILITIES - Category 2	
Accounts Payable	200
Unearned Revenue	205
Bank Loan	210
Equipment Loan	215
OWNER'S EQUITY - Category 3	
Capital Account	300
Owner's Drawings	310
Income Summary	315

Account Description	Account #
REVENUE - Category 4	
Sales	400
EXPENSES - Category 5	
Advertising	500
Bad Debts	505
Insurance	510
Maintenance	515
Miscellaneous	520
Office Supplies	525
Professional Fees	530
Rent	535
Salaries and Bonuses	540
Salary Benefits	541
Telephone	545
Travel	550
Depreciation	555
OTHER REVENUE & EXPENSES	
Interest Earned on Savings	600
Discounts Received	605
Interest & Bank Charges	700

DATE	DESCRIPTION	GL NO.	DR	CR

Complete the general ledgers.

ACCOUNT: *CASH*				No. 101
DATE	**DESCRIPTION**	**DR**	**CR**	**BALANCE (DR or CR)**

ACCOUNT:				No.
DATE	**DESCRIPTION**	**DR**	**CR**	**BALANCE (DR or CR)**

ACCOUNT:				No.
DATE	**DESCRIPTION**	**DR**	**CR**	**BALANCE (DR or CR)**

ACCOUNT:				No.
DATE	**DESCRIPTION**	**DR**	**CR**	**BALANCE (DR or CR)**

ACCOUNT:				No.
DATE	**DESCRIPTION**	**DR**	**CR**	**BALANCE (DR or CR)**

ACCOUNT:				No.
DATE	**DESCRIPTION**	**DR**	**CR**	**BALANCE (DR or CR)**

ACCOUNT:				No.
DATE	**DESCRIPTION**	**DR**	**CR**	**BALANCE (DR or CR)**

ACCOUNT:				No.
DATE	DESCRIPTION	DR	CR	BALANCE (DR or CR)

ACCOUNT:				No.
DATE	DESCRIPTION	DR	CR	BALANCE (DR or CR)

Complete the trial balance worksheet for question 2.

DENVIC REPAIRS INC. - TRIAL BALANCE - WORKSHEET - FOR THE MONTH ENDING JUNE 30, 2010							
		TRIAL BALANCE		INCOME STATEMENT		BALANCE SHEET	
#	ACCOUNT TITLE	DR	CR	DR	CR	DR	CR
	Totals						
	NET INCOME (LOSS)						
	Allocated Net Income (Loss) to Balance Sheet						
	TOTAL						

Complete the formal financial statements for question 2.

Denvic Repairs Inc. Income Statement For the Month Ending June 30, 2010		

Denvic Repairs Inc. Statement Of Owner's Equity For the Month Ending June 30, 2010		

Denvic Repairs Inc. Balance Sheet As at June 30, 2010			
Assets		**Liabilities**	

Question 3

The chart of accounts and a list of transactions from Woodrow & Company are shown below. Prepare the general journal entries to record these transactions, post them to the general ledger, and complete the trial balance worksheet. In addition, create the income statement, balance sheet and statement of owner's equity.

Use this Chart of Accounts:

Account Description	Account #
ASSETS - Category 1	
Cash	101
Accounts Receivable	105
Prepaid Expenses	110
Inventory	115
Fixed Assets - Equipment	120
Accumulated Depreciation	130
LIABILITIES - Category 2	
Accounts Payable	200
Unearned Revenue	205
Bank Loan	210
Equipment Loan	215
OWNER'S EQUITY - Category 3	
Capital Account	300
Owner's Drawings	310
Income Summary	315

Account Description	Account #
REVENUE - Category 4	
Sales	400
EXPENSES - Category 5	
Advertising	500
Bad Debts	505
Insurance	510
Maintenance	515
Miscellaneous	520
Office Supplies	525
Professional Fees	530
Rent	535
Salaries and Bonuses	540
Salary Benefits	541
Telephone	545
Travel	550
Depreciation	555
OTHER REVENUE & EXPENSES	
Interest Earned on Savings	600
Discounts Received	605
Interest & Bank Charges	700

Transactions for the month of December:

Dec 1	Owner deposited cash into the business in the form of owner's equity to capitalize the business	$30,000
Dec 1	Borrowed cash from the bank	10,000
Dec 2	Bought furniture and computers (equipment) with cash	8,000
Dec 3	Received cash for services provided	15,000
Dec 5	Paid rent for the month with cash	1,100
Dec 15	Paid employee salaries	6,000
Dec 15	Paid interest on loan	200
Dec 17	Paid maintenance expense	500
Dec 17	Telephone expenses to be paid next month	300
Dec 18	Recorded travel expenses charged on account - to be paid next month	2,000
Dec 22	Prepaid insurance for one year	6,000
Dec 22	Paid portion of bank loan principal	3,000

Dec 23	The owner drew cash for personal use	2,000
Adjustments		
Dec 31	Recognized prepaid insurance for one month as an expense	500
Dec 31	Recorded depreciation of furniture and computers (equipment)	400

DATE	DESCRIPTION	GL NO.	DR	CR

DATE	DESCRIPTION	GL NO.	DR	CR

Prepare the general ledgers.

ACCOUNT: *CASH*				No. 101
DATE	**DESCRIPTION**	**DR**	**CR**	**BALANCE (DR or CR)**

ACCOUNT:				No.
DATE	**DESCRIPTION**	**DR**	**CR**	**BALANCE (DR or CR)**

ACCOUNT:				No.
DATE	**DESCRIPTION**	**DR**	**CR**	**BALANCE (DR or CR)**

ACCOUNT:				No.
DATE	**DESCRIPTION**	**DR**	**CR**	**BALANCE (DR or CR)**

ACCOUNT:				No.
DATE	**DESCRIPTION**	**DR**	**CR**	**BALANCE (DR or CR)**

ACCOUNT:				No.
DATE	**DESCRIPTION**	**DR**	**CR**	**BALANCE (DR or CR)**

ACCOUNT: No.

DATE	DESCRIPTION	DR	CR	BALANCE (DR or CR)

ACCOUNT: No.

DATE	DESCRIPTION	DR	CR	BALANCE (DR or CR)

ACCOUNT: No.

DATE	DESCRIPTION	DR	CR	BALANCE (DR or CR)

ACCOUNT: No.

DATE	DESCRIPTION	DR	CR	BALANCE (DR or CR)

ACCOUNT: No.

DATE	DESCRIPTION	DR	CR	BALANCE (DR or CR)

ACCOUNT: No.

DATE	DESCRIPTION	DR	CR	BALANCE (DR or CR)

ACCOUNT: No.

DATE	DESCRIPTION	DR	CR	BALANCE (DR or CR)

ACCOUNT: No.

DATE	DESCRIPTION	DR	CR	BALANCE (DR or CR)

ACCOUNT: No.

DATE	DESCRIPTION	DR	CR	BALANCE (DR or CR)

ACCOUNT: No.

DATE	DESCRIPTION	DR	CR	BALANCE (DR or CR)

Complete the trial balance worksheet for question 3.

WOODROW & COMPANY – TRIAL BALANCE – WORKSHEET – FOR THE MONTH ENDING DECEMBER 31, 2010											
		UNADJUSTED TRIAL BALANCE		ADJUSTMENTS		ADJUSTED TRIAL BALANCE		INCOME STATEMENT		BALANCE SHEET	
#	ACCOUNT TITLES	DR	CR	DR	CR	DR	CR	DR	CR	DR	CR
	Totals										
	Adjustments										
	Total Adjusted										
	Net Income (Loss)										
	Allocated Net Income (Loss) to Balance Sheet										
	TOTAL										

Complete the formal financial statements for question 3.

WOODROW & COMPANY INCOME STATEMENT FOR THE MONTH ENDING DECEMBER 31, 2010	

WOODROW & COMPANY STATEMENT OF OWNER'S EQUITY FOR THE MONTH ENDING DECEMBER 31, 2010	

WOODROW & COMPANY BALANCE SHEET AS AT DECEMBER 31, 2010	

Question 4

A list of transactions for e-Mark Industries inc. and the chart of accounts are shown below. Complete the accounting cycle for the month of June 2010.

Jun 1	Received cash from sales	$6,300
Jun 1	Charged travel expenses on account	2,500
Jun 1	Paid cash for maintenance expenses	1,000
Jun 1	Bought a computer - to be paid next month	1,500
Jun 1	Paid staff salaries	2,000
Jun 8	Borrowed cash from the bank	3,000
Jun 10	Paid interest on bank loan	200
Jun 10	Paid a portion of bank loan principal	500
Jun 15	Depreciated equipment	500
Jun 15	Paid additional interest on bank loan	100
Jun 15	Paid cash for monthly rent expenses	2,200
Jun 15	Paid cash for telephone expenses	150
Jun 16	Received interest on a company savings account	80
Jun 17	Paid cash for car insurance	500
Jun 19	Sold long-term assets for cash (book value)	800
Jun 21	Charged a newspaper advertisement on account	450
Jun 22	Received a lawyer's invoice for services rendered	950
Jun 26	Paid cash for miscellaneous expenses	400
Jun 28	Paid cash towards accounts payable	1,300

- Assume the opening balances are zero
- Record the transactions in the general journal
- Post the general journal to the general ledger
- Prepare the worksheet for the month ended June 30, 2010
- Prepare the financial statements for the month

Account Description	Account #
ASSETS - Category 1	
Cash	101
Accounts Receivable	105
Prepaid Expenses	110
Inventory	115
Fixed Assets - Equipment	120
Accumulated Depreciation	130
LIABILITIES - Category 2	
Accounts Payable	200
Unearned Revenue	205
Bank Loan	210
Equipment Loan	215
OWNER'S EQUITY - Category 3	
Capital Account	300
Owner's Drawings	310
Income Summary	315

Account Description	Account #
REVENUE - Category 4	
Sales	400
EXPENSES - Category 5	
Advertising	500
Bad Debts	505
Insurance	510
Maintenance	515
Miscellaneous	520
Office Supplies	525
Professional Fees	530
Rent	535
Salaries and Bonuses	540
Salary Benefits	541
Telephone	545
Travel	550
Depreciation	555
OTHER REVENUE & EXPENSES	
Interest Earned on Savings	600
Discounts Received	605
Interest & Bank Charges	700

DATE	DESCRIPTION	GL NO.	DR	CR

DATE	DESCRIPTION	GL NO.	DR	CR

DATE	DESCRIPTION	GL NO.	DR	CR

ACCOUNT: *CASH*				No. *101*
DATE	**DESCRIPTION**	**DR**	**CR**	**BALANCE (DR or CR)**

ACCOUNT: *LONG-TERM ASSETS - EQUIPMENT*				No. *120*
DATE	**DESCRIPTION**	**DR**	**CR**	**BALANCE (DR or CR)**

ACCOUNT: *ACCOUNTS PAYABLE*				No. *200*
DATE	**DESCRIPTION**	**DR**	**CR**	**BALANCE (DR or CR)**

ACCOUNT: *BANK LOAN*				No. *210*
DATE	**DESCRIPTION**	**DR**	**CR**	**BALANCE (DR or CR)**

ACCOUNT: *SALES*				No. *400*
DATE	**DESCRIPTION**	**DR**	**CR**	**BALANCE (DR or CR)**

ACCOUNT: *ADVERTISING*				No. *500*
DATE	**DESCRIPTION**	**DR**	**CR**	**BALANCE (DR or CR)**

ACCOUNT: *INSURANCE*				No. *510*
DATE	**DESCRIPTION**	**DR**	**CR**	**BALANCE (DR or CR)**

ACCOUNT: *MAINTENANCE*				No. *515*
DATE	**DESCRIPTION**	**DR**	**CR**	**BALANCE (DR or CR)**

ACCOUNT: *MISCELLANEOUS*				No. *520*
DATE	**DESCRIPTION**	**DR**	**CR**	**BALANCE (DR or CR)**

ACCOUNT: *PROFESSIONAL FEES*				No. *530*
DATE	**DESCRIPTION**	**DR**	**CR**	**BALANCE (DR or CR)**

ACCOUNT: *RENT*				No. *535*
DATE	**DESCRIPTION**	**DR**	**CR**	**BALANCE (DR or CR)**

ACCOUNT: *SALARIES AND BONUSES*				No. *540*
DATE	**DESCRIPTION**	**DR**	**CR**	**BALANCE (DR or CR)**

ACCOUNT: *TELEPHONE*				No. *545*
DATE	**DESCRIPTION**	**DR**	**CR**	**BALANCE (DR or CR)**

ACCOUNT: *TRAVEL*				No. *550*
DATE	**DESCRIPTION**	**DR**	**CR**	**BALANCE (DR or CR)**

ACCOUNT: *DEPRECIATION*				No. *555*
DATE	**DESCRIPTION**	**DR**	**CR**	**BALANCE (DR or CR)**

ACCOUNT: *INTEREST EARNED ON SAVINGS*				No. *600*
DATE	**DESCRIPTION**	**DR**	**CR**	**BALANCE (DR or CR)**

ACCOUNT: *INTEREST AND BANK CHARGES*				No. *700*
DATE	**DESCRIPTION**	**DR**	**CR**	**BALANCE (DR or CR)**

E-MARK INDUSTRIES - TRIAL BALANCE WORKSHEET - FOR THE MONTH ENDING JUNE 30, 2010							
		TRIAL BALANCE		**INCOME STATEMENT**		**BALANCE SHEET**	
#	**ACCOUNT TITLES**	**DR**	**CR**	**DR**	**CR**	**DR**	**CR**
	Totals						
	NET INCOME (LOSS)						
	Allocated Net Income (Loss) to Balance Sheet						
	TOTAL						

E-MARK INDUSTRIES INCOME STATEMENT FOR THE MONTH ENDING JUNE 30, 2010	

E-MARK INDUSTRIES STATEMENT OF OWNER'S EQUITY FOR THE MONTH ENDING JUNE 30, 2010	

E-MARK INDUSTRIES
BALANCE SHEET
AS AT JUNE 30, 2010

Question 5

Part 1

The trial balance for Woodsworth Academy is shown below:

Woodsworth Academy Trial Balance Month ending June 30, 2010		
ACCOUNT TITLES	**DR**	**CR**
Cash	38,000	
Accounts Receivable	12,000	
Prepaid Insurance	11,000	
Land	58,000	
Accounts Payable		11,100
Bank Loans Payable		46,500
Capital		50,500
Owner's Drawings	2,000	
Revenue		19,500
Salaries Expense	3,500	
Insurance Expense	1,200	
Interest Expense	600	
Utilities Expense	500	
Advertising	800	
Total	**127,600**	**127,600**

1. Prepare the journal entries to close the books. Assume the company uses the income summary account.

DATE	DESCRIPTION	DR	CR

2. Prepare the post-closing trial balance for the company.

Woodsworth Academy Post-Closing Trial Balance Month ending June 30, 2010		
ACCOUNT TITLES	**DR**	**CR**
Total		

Part 2

The trial balance for Woodsworth Academy is shown below:

Woodsworth Academy Trial Balance Month ending June 30, 2010		
ACCOUNT TITLES	**DR**	**CR**
Cash	24,200	
Accounts Receivable	9,000	
Prepaid Insurance	5,400	
Land	13,000	
Accounts Payable		14,800
Bank Loans Payable		5,000
Capital		34,500
Owner's Drawings	2,000	
Revenue		5,900
Salaries Expense	4,600	
Insurance Expense	500	
Interest Expense	600	
Utilities Expense	200	
Advertising	700	
Total	**60,200**	**60,200**

1. Prepare the journal entries to close the books. Assume the company records closing entries directly to the owner's capital account.

DATE	DESCRIPTION	DR	CR

2. Prepare the post-closing trial balance for the company.

Woodsworth Academy Post-Closing Trial Balance Month ending June 30, 2010		
ACCOUNT TITLES	**DR**	**CR**
Total		

Part 3

The trial balance for Woodsworth academy is shown below:

Woodsworth Academy Trial Balance Month ending February 28, 2010		
ACCOUNT TITLES	**DR**	**CR**
Cash	60,000	
Accounts Receivable	10,400	
Prepaid Insurance	600	
Land	80,000	
Accounts Payable		7,600
Bank Loans Payable		85,000
Capital		58,400
Revenue		15,200
Salaries Expense	6,000	
Insurance Expense	800	
Interest Expense	2,200	
Utilities Expense	400	
Advertising	5,800	
Total	**166,200**	**166,200**

1. Prepare the journal entries to close the books. Assume the company uses the income summary account.

DATE	DESCRIPTION	DR	CR

2. Prepare the post-closing trial balance for the company. Did ending capital balance increase, decrease or remain the same? Why?

Woodsworth Academy Post-Closing Trial Balance Month ending February 28, 2010		
ACCOUNT TITLES	**DR**	**CR**
Total		

Chapter 5

MERCHANDISING OPERATIONS

Assessment Questions

Question 1

Explain how the owner's equity account in a corporation is different from that of a proprietorship.

Question 2

Describe the three different ways in which revenue can be recognized.

Question 3

Define gross profit margin.

Question 4

Describe the differences between a perpetual and periodic inventory system.

Question 5

List the three different ways in which an expense can be recognized.

Question 6

What is a contra account? Why is it used when preparing financial statements?

Question 7

Explain why arranging a loan has no impact on equity.

Question 8

Explain the difference between current and long-term debt.

Application Questions

Question 1

a) Deanna Colin contributed $100,000 to a new business operating as a corporation called Cosea Limited. Prepare the journal entry for the company to record the investment.

DATE	DESCRIPTION	DR	CR

b) Deanna negotiated a bank loan in the amount of $50,000, payable in equal annual installments over the next five years. Prepare the journal entry and be mindful of the current portion and long-term portion of the loan.

DATE	DESCRIPTION	DR	CR

c) The company purchased equipment with $20,000 cash. Prepare the journal entry to record the purchase.

DATE	DESCRIPTION	DR	CR

d) The company also purchased inventory in the amount of $60,000 with cash. Prepare the journal entry to record the inventory purchase.

DATE	DESCRIPTION	DR	CR

e) The company sold $50,000 worth of inventory for $80,000 on account. Prepare the journal entry to record the sale.

DATE	DESCRIPTION	DR	CR

f) The company paid $1,200 in advance for insurance coverage for one year. The insurance premium is $100 per month. Prepare the journal entry to record the prepayment.

DATE	DESCRIPTION	DR	CR

During the month, various expenses were incurred. Record the following transactions:

g) Travel expenses were incurred in the amount of $3,000, to be paid next month.

DATE	DESCRIPTION	DR	CR

h) Salaries were paid with cash in the amount of $18,000.

DATE	DESCRIPTION	DR	CR

i) Rent was paid with cash in the amount of $5,000.

DATE	DESCRIPTION	DR	CR

At the end of the month, various adjustments were made. Record the following transactions:

j) Recognized $100 of prepaid insurance as an expense.

DATE	DESCRIPTION	DR	CR

k) Refer to transaction (c), the equipment purchased for $20,000 should be depreciated over a 5-year period. Prepare the journal entry to record depreciation for the month.

DATE	DESCRIPTION	DR	CR

l) The company cancelled the insurance policy and received a refund of $1,100. Record the journal entry for this transaction.

DATE	DESCRIPTION	DR	CR

There were a few more transactions for the month relating to the payment of outstanding debts and the collection of accounts receivable. Record the following transaction:

m) A portion of the outstanding bank loan was paid: $10,000 of principal and $500 of interest.

DATE	DESCRIPTION	DR	CR

n) Accounts receivable were collected in the amount of $30,000.

DATE	DESCRIPTION	DR	CR

o) Accounts payable were reduced by $3,000.

DATE	DESCRIPTION	DR	CR

Question 2

a) On April 1, 2010, William M. Wilcoxen and Jerry Bryant incorporated W-B Limited and each contributed $50,000 cash. Prepare the journal entries for W–B Limited to record the new investments.

DATE	DESCRIPTION	DR	CR
Apr 1			

b) On the same day, W–B Limited then negotiated a loan with a bank for $40,000, payable in 4 equal installments over the next four years. Prepare the journal entry to record the receipt of the bank loan.

DATE	DESCRIPTION	DR	CR
Apr 1			

c) When the bank loaned W–B Limited the cash, it demanded collateral. Since W-B Limited had no assets at the time of the loan, Wilcoxen and Bryant had to offer personal assets as collateral. List three examples of items that Wilcoxen and Bryant could use as collateral and why they would be used.

d) The bank loan of $40,000 is payable in equal annual installments over four years. Complete the following chart for the amount owing at the end of the first two years after the payments have been made (March 31, 2011 and March 31, 2012).

	March 31, 2011	March 31, 2012
Current Debt		
Long-term debt		

e) W-B Limited purchased a machine with $75,000 cash. Prepare the journal entry to record the purchase.

DATE	DESCRIPTION	DR	CR

f) W-B Limited purchased $10,000 worth of inventory with cash. Prepare the journal entry to record the inventory purchase.

DATE	DESCRIPTION	DR	CR

g) At the end of the first year of operation, W–B Limited generated cash sales of $390,000 and their expenses amounted to $380,000 (assume zero taxes). Calculate the following: (1) the net income amount for the first year; and (2) the amount of stockholder's equity at the end of the first year. The stockholders' equity at the beginning of the year was $100,000.

h) Prepare a balance sheet (as at year-end March 31, 2011) using the transactions from questions 1 to 7. Assume the first loan installment has been paid.

W-B Limited Balance Sheet As at March 31, 2011	
Assets	
Current Assets	
Long-Term Assets	
Total Assets	
Liabilities	
Current Liabilities	
Long-Term Liabilities	
Total Liabilities	
Stockholders' Equity	
Liabilities + Stockholders' Equity	

Question 3

Record the following transactions in the journal provided.

Transactions:

1.	Deposited an advance payment from a customer	$5,000
2	Sold your services for cash	3,000
3.	Billed customer for services rendered - they will pay next month	5,000
4.	Recognized unearned revenue as earned	2,000
5.	Paid various cash expenses	6,000

After recording each transaction, indicate whether cash increased ("INC"), decreased ("DEC"), or stayed the same ("SAME"). Then repeat this part of the exercise for any change in equity.

DATE	DESCRIPTION	DR	CR	Change in Cash	Change in Equity

Question 4

Record the following transactions in the journal provided.

Transactions:

1.	Sold your services for cash	$10,000
2	Prepaid insurance for the year in advance	6,000
3.	Paid cash for miscellaneous expenses	1,500
4.	Charged this month's advertising expenses to the company credit card	2,000
5.	Recognized prepaid insurance for the month	500

After recording each transaction, indicate whether cash increased ("INC"), decreased ("DEC"), or stayed the same ("SAME"). Then repeat this part of the exercise for any change in equity.

DATE	DESCRIPTION	DR	CR	Change in Cash	Change in Equity

Question 5

Place an 'x' under the correct column to show whether the following transactions cause an increase, decrease, or no change to cash in the bank and equity. Also enter the new cash balance and owner's equity value after each transaction. We have completed an example for you.

			Cash				Equity			
	Transaction	Amount	Increase	Decrease	No Change	Cash Balance	Increase	Decrease	No Change	Equity Balance
	Opening Balances					$0				$0
	Made cash sales	$15,000	x			15,000	x			15,000
1	Invested personal funds in business	120,000								
2	Deposited bank loan	60,000								
3	Purchased long-term assets with cash	140,000								
4	Prepaid insurance for 12 months	6,000								
5	Deposited unearned revenue	15,000								
6	Bought inventory - to be paid next month	60,000								
7	Paid salaries & benefits with cash	12,000								
8	Paid advertising costs with cash	2,000								
9	Paid cash for rent	3,000								
10	Recorded depreciation of long-term assets	2,000								
11	Paid for miscellaneous expenses	4,000								
12	Recognized unearned revenue as earned	10,000								
13	Recorded maintenance fees (to be paid next month)	7,000								
14	Sales on account (will collect next month)	90,000								
15	Recorded the cost of goods sold	72,000								

Question 6

Enter the new cash balance and owner's equity value for each transaction on the chart below. Write either the "+" or "-" amount or "no change". We have completed an example for you.

	Transaction	Change to Cash Balance	Change to Owner's Equity
	Record cash sales of $3,000 (COGS is $2,000)	+ 3,000	+ 1,000
1	Sell product for $10,000 (cost is $8,000) - customer will pay next month		
2	Sell services for $600 cash		
3	Give away $400 worth of product for free		
4	Deposit unearned revenue of $1,000 from a customer		
5	Recognize $500 of unearned revenue as earned		
6	Refund a deposit of $600 to a customer because you were not able to deliver the product as promised		
7	Sell product for $6,000 (cost is $4,000) - the customer pays $1,000 now and promises to pay the balance next month		
8	Collect $500 of outstanding accounts receivable owning from a customer		
9	Deliver services for $1,000 - the customer prepaid this amount to you last month		
10	Sell products for $800 that cost you $600 - the customer pays cash		

Question 7

Complete the following charts to determine the cost of goods sold, the gross profit and gross profit margin.

1.

Item	Amount
Sales	$250,000
Opening inventory	120,000
Purchases for the period	30,000
Closing inventory	40,000
Cost of goods sold	
Gross profit	
Gross profit margin	

2.

Item	Amount
Sales	$150,000
Opening Inventory	110,000
Purchases for the period	25,000
Closing inventory	42,000
Cost of goods sold	
Gross profit	
Gross profit margin	

3. Explain the difference between a perpetual and a periodic inventory system.

____

____

____

Question 8

Catherine Stromain and Maggie Jones operate a small importing company. During the month of January, the following transactions occurred:

Jan 4	Purchased 300 clocks with cash	$3,000
Jan 5	Paid freight on the clock shipment from Jan 4	300
Jan 7	Sold 100 clocks on account	1,500
Jan 7	Record the cost of clocks sold	1,100
Jan 10	Collected outstanding accounts receivable	4,000
Jan 15	Purchased 100 mirrors - to be paid later	3,000
Jan 17	Received advanced payment from a customer for 100 mirrors to be shipped later	6,000

Required:
Journalize the transactions in the worksheets provided.

DATE	DESCRIPTION	DR	CR

Calculate the gross profit for the month of January.

Calculate the gross profit margin for the month of January.

Question 9

George K. Connor operates a company that sells goods and services. During the month, the following transactions occurred.

Date	Details	Amount
Feb 1	Received a deposit from a customer for services to be provided later	$6,000
Feb 1	Prepaid insurance for one year	3,600
Feb 3	Sold services for cash	4,000
Feb 5	Sent invoice to a customer for services performed	6,000
Feb 7	Recognized unearned revenue as earned	3,000
Feb 11	Paid various cash expenses	200
Feb 16	Recorded advertising services on account	3,000
Feb 20	Purchased inventory - to be paid later	36,000
Feb 21	Sold products on account	31,000
Feb 21	Recorded COGS for products sold	14,000
Feb 22	Paid wages and benefits	6,000
Feb 25	Purchased new computers - to be paid later	4,000
Feb 26	Incurred maintenance expense - to be paid next month	2,000
Feb 27	Customers paid their outstanding account balances owing	3,000
Feb 28	Recognized prepaid insurance for one month	300

Required:

Prepare the journal entries for the period.
Post the entries to the general ledger.
Prepare a trial balance.
Prepare an income statement for the period.
Prepare a balance sheet for the period.
Calculate the gross profit margin on product sales.

Note: use the chart of accounts from the review exercise.

DATE	DESCRIPTION	GL NO.	DR	CR

DATE	DESCRIPTION	GL NO.	DR	CR

ACCOUNT: *CASH*				No. 101
DATE	**DESCRIPTION**	**DR**	**CR**	**BALANCE (DR or CR)**

ACCOUNT: *ACCOUNTS RECEIVABLE*				No. 105
DATE	**DESCRIPTION**	**DR**	**CR**	**BALANCE (DR or CR)**

ACCOUNT: *PREPAID EXPENSES*				No. 110
DATE	**DESCRIPTION**	**DR**	**CR**	**BALANCE (DR or CR)**

ACCOUNT: *INVENTORY*				No. 115
DATE	**DESCRIPTION**	**DR**	**CR**	**BALANCE (DR or CR)**

ACCOUNT: LONG-TERM – EQUIPMENT				No. 120
DATE	**DESCRIPTION**	**DR**	**CR**	**BALANCE (DR or CR)**

ACCOUNT: *ACCOUNTS PAYABLE*				No. 200
DATE	**DESCRIPTION**	**DR**	**CR**	**BALANCE (DR or CR)**

ACCOUNT: *UNEARNED REVENUE*				No. 205
DATE	**DESCRIPTION**	**DR**	**CR**	**BALANCE (DR or CR)**

ACCOUNT: *REVENUE*				No. 400
DATE	**DESCRIPTION**	**DR**	**CR**	**BALANCE (DR or CR)**

ACCOUNT: *COST OF GOODS SOLD*				No. 500
DATE	**DESCRIPTION**	**DR**	**CR**	**BALANCE (DR or CR)**

ACCOUNT: *ADVERTISING*				No. 501
DATE	**DESCRIPTION**	**DR**	**CR**	**BALANCE (DR or CR)**

ACCOUNT: *MISCELLANEOUS EXPENSE*				No. 520
DATE	**DESCRIPTION**	**DR**	**CR**	**BALANCE (DR or CR)**

ACCOUNT: *SALARIES AND BENEFITS*				No. 540
DATE	**DESCRIPTION**	**DR**	**CR**	**BALANCE (DR or CR)**

ACCOUNT: *MAINTENANCE*				No. 515
DATE	**DESCRIPTION**	**DR**	**CR**	**BALANCE (DR or CR)**

ACCOUNT: *INSURANCE*				No. 510
DATE	**DESCRIPTION**	**DR**	**CR**	**BALANCE (DR or CR)**

GEORGE K. CONNOR - TRIAL BALANCE - WORKSHEET - FOR PERIOD ENDING FEBRUARY 28, 2011						
	TRIAL BALANCE		**INCOME STATEMENT**		**BALANCE SHEET**	
ACCOUNT TITLES	**DR**	**CR**	**DR**	**CR**	**DR**	**CR**
Totals						
NET INCOME (LOSS)						
Allocated Net Income to the Balance Sheet						
TOTAL						

GEORGE K. CONNOR INCOME STATEMENT FOR THE MONTH ENDING FEBRUARY 28, 2011	
Sales of Product	
Sales of Service	
Total Revenue	
Less: COGS	
Gross Profit	
Expenses	
Total Expenses	
Net Income (Loss)	

Calculate the gross profit margin on product sales.

____

____

GEORGE K. CONNOR BALANCE SHEET FOR THE MONTH ENDING FEBRUARY 28, 2011	
ASSETS	
Total Assets	
LIABILITIES	
Total Liabilities	
OWNER'S EQUITY	
LIABILITIES + OWNER'S EQUITY	

Question 10

Part of the trial balance for Greg's Cottage Ltd. on June 30, 2009 is shown below:

Account Title	DR	CR
Cash	$19,600	
Prepaid Insurance	4,500	
Office Supplies	2,600	

Additional information:

i) The balance in prepaid insurance is a one-year premium paid on April 1, 2009.

ii) A physical count shows $450 of office supplies are still on hand by June 30, 2009.

Required:

a) Prepare the journal entry to record the adjustment for prepaid insurance as at June 30, 2009.

DATE	DESCRIPTION	DR	CR

b) Prepare the journal entry to record the adjustment for office supplies as at June 30, 2009.

DATE	DESCRIPTION	DR	CR

c) What would the balances be for cash, prepaid insurance, and office supplies after the adjustments were made?

Account Title	DR	CR

Critical Thinking

Jimmy Cricket is the bookkeeper for Pinocchio Enterprises Inc. (PEI). For the period ending March 31, 2011, PEI experienced a net profit (assume no taxes) of $300,000. A few months later, however, Jimmy Cricket was reviewing the long-term asset account and found that he forgot to record depreciation for a piece of machinery bought on November 1st, 2010 for $60,000. The machine is expected to last 5 years with no residual value. Was net profit for the period ending March 31, 2011 over-stated or under-stated? By how much?

Notes

Chapter 6

CASH AND SHORT-TERM INVESTMENTS

Assessment Questions

Question 1

Define short-term investments.

Question 2

Why do businesses make short-term investments?

Question 3

Describe the position of short-term investments on the Statement of Financial Position (balance sheet). Explain the placement of short-term investments.

Question 4

Name the two main types of short-term investments, and give a brief description of each.

Question 5

Differentiate interest revenue from dividend revenue.

Question 6

Name three examples of marketable securities.

Question 7

A company issues bonds with interest payable on April 30 and October 31 of each year. How does this fact affect the purchaser when the bond is purchased between the above dates?

Question 8

A company purchases some bonds, paying less than par (face) value. What is the term used to describe the difference between the face value and the amount paid? How does the purchaser deal with the difference?

Question 9

What are "other assets"? Explain.

Application Questions

Question 1

Quality Electronic Corporation is preparing a bank reconciliation and has identified the following potential reconciling items. For each item, indicate if it is (i) added to the balance per ledger, (ii) deducted from the balance per ledger, (iii) added to the balance per bank statement, (iv) deducted from the balance per bank statement.

a) Deposits that are not shown on the bank statement
b) Interest credited to the company's account
c) Bank service charges
d) Outstanding checks
e) NSF checks returned

Question 2

The following data represents information necessary to assist in preparing the June 30th bank reconciliation for Trimore Company Inc.

a) The June 30th bank balance was $5,300
b) The bank statement indicated a deduction of $30 for bank service charges
c) A customer deposited $1,200 directly into the bank account to settle an outstanding accounts receivable bill
d) Check numbers 850 for $600 and check number 857 for $420 have been recorded in the company ledger but did not appear on the bank statement
e) A customer paid an amount of $4,534 to Trimore on the 30th of June but the deposit did not appear on the bank statement
f) The accounting clerk made an error and recorded a $200 check as $2,000. The check was written to pay outstanding accounts payable account

g) A check number 9574 for $100 was deducted from Trimore's account by the bank. This check was not written by Trimore and needs to be reversed by the bank.

h) The bank included an NSF check in the amount of $820 relating to a customers payment.

i) The General Ledger cash account showed a balance of $6,764 on June 30th

Required:

1. Complete the bank reconciliation for Trimore Manufacturers
2. Write the necessary journal entries to correct Trimore's records

		Bank	Ledger

DATE	DESCRIPTION	DR	CR

DATE	DESCRIPTION	DR	CR

DATE	DESCRIPTION	DR	CR

DATE	DESCRIPTION	DR	CR

Question 3

a) Prepare the July reconciliation statement for World's Computer Inc. using the following information

- Cash balance per general ledger is $2,219
- Bank statement balance is $2,478.80
- These checks were recorded in the cash payments journal but did not appear on the bank statement. They are: Check #186 for $100; Check #193 for $57; Check #199 for $143.
- A deposit for $368 dated July 31 was recorded in the cash receipts journal but did not appear on the bank statement
- Service charges of $18 are shown on the bank statement
- A check for $37.50 has been cashed (correctly) by the bank but was incorrectly recorded in the company's cash payments journal as $375.50. The check was issued for the purchase of office supplies.
- The bank automatically deposited interest of $7.80 at the end of the month.

b) In a general journal, record any entries required to bring the company records up to date.

a)

World's Computer Inc. Bank Reconciliation Statement July 31, 2008		
	Ledger	**Bank**

b)

Date	Description	DR	CR

Question 4

Mike's Cleaning Service received its monthly bank statement for its business bank account, with a balance of $55,062 for the month of July 2011. The total for the ledger account at the date was $59,461. After a comparison of the checks written by the company and those deducted from the bank account, Mike's accountant determined that three checks, totaling $2,806 (No. 256 - $606, No. 261 - $1,200, No. 262 - $1,000), were outstanding on July 31. A review of the deposits showed that a deposit on July 1 for $12,610 was actually recorded in the company's ledger on June 30 and a July 31 deposit of $9,760 was recorded in the company's ledger on the date but had not been recorded by the bank yet. The July bank statement showed a service fee of $18, a customer's check in the amount of $70 that had been returned NSF, a loan payment of $857 that was deducted automatically by the bank, and a note for $3,500 that was collected by the bank for Mike's Cleaning Service.

Required:

a) Prepare the bank reconciliation at July 31.

b) How much cash does Mike's Cleaning Service actually have in its cash account at July 31?

c) Prepare adjusting journal entries to record all necessary adjustments to bring the cash account to its adjusted balance.

a)

Mike's Cleaning Service Bank Reconciliation Statement July 31, 2011		
	Ledger	**Bank**

b) ____________________

c)

DATE	DESCRIPTION	DR	CR

Question 5

On June 7, Mary decided to use a petty cash fund for her small business. A check of $125 was issued and cashed. The $125 cash was given to the store supervisor who was to act as petty cashier. The petty cashier was told to obtain authorized vouchers for all payments. Petty cash was to be replenished when the balance in the cash box reached $23.

a) Record the establishment of the fund on June 7.

b) On June 19, this summary was prepared:

Delivery Expense	$50.90
Miscellaneous Expense	20.40
Office Expense	24.10
Postage Expense	6.60
Total	102

Prepare the entry to replenish the petty cash.

c) On June 23, it was decided to increase the amount of the petty cash fund from $125 to $175. A check of $50 was issued. Record the transaction.

a)

DATE	DESCRIPTION	DR	CR

b)

DATE	DESCRIPTION	DR	CR

c)

DATE	DESCRIPTION	DR	CR

Question 6

The petty cash fund was established on August 12, 2011 in the amount of $250.00. Expenditures from the fund by the custodian as of August 31, 2011, were evidenced by approved receipts for the following

Postage expense	$30
Supplies expense	65
Employee payable	42
Shipping charges	58.20
Newspaper advertising expense	21.95
Miscellaneous expense	15.75

On August 31, 2011, the petty cash fund was replenished and increased to $300.00; currency and coin in the fund at that time totaled $15.60.

Required:

Prepare the journal entries to record the transactions related to the petty cash fund for the month of August.

DATE	DESCRIPTION	DR	CR

DATE	DESCRIPTION	DR	CR

DATE	DESCRIPTION	DR	CR

Question 7

Last year, Holtzman Company established a petty cash fund of $100. The custodian complained that she had to reimburse the fund on a weekly basis, and suggested that the fund be increased to $400. That way, she would only have to summarize payouts and get a check from the cashier once per month.

Management agreed with the custodian, and advised the cashier to increase the fund to $400.

a) Write the journal entry to increase the fund to $400.

b) List at least five internal controls that should be established around the use of petty cash.

a)

DATE	DESCRIPTION	DR	CR

b) ______________________________

Question 8

On March 30th, Skyline Enterprises established a $300 petty cash fund.

a) Prepare the entry to record the establishment of the fund.

b) At the end of the month, the petty cash custodian analyzed all the monthly transactions. She opened the petty cash box and counted $100 cash remaining. There were also two receipts in the petty cash box: receipt # 1: $100 – Entertainment and receipt #2: $98 – Travel. Record the journal entries for this month's expenses and replenish the fund.

c) At the end of the month, Skyline Enterprises wanted to increase the petty cash fund by $100. Prepare the journal entry to record the increase in petty cash fund.

a)

DATE	DESCRIPTION	DR	CR

b)

DATE	DESCRIPTION	DR	CR

c)

DATE	DESCRIPTION	DR	CR

Question 9

Julio Ivors operates a proprietorship. Sales have been very good in recent months, resulting in a substantial amount of cash on hand. However, Julio knows that in six months, he will have to purchase more inventory for the next season. He realizes that if he leaves the cash in the bank, he will receive an insignificant amount of interest. He, therefore, decides to loan his excess cash of $20,000 to his brother-in-law, charging interest at annual rate of 12%. Assume Julio Ivors has a year-end of December 31.

Required:

1. Record the entry when issuing the loan on August 15
2. Record any required entries related to the loan as of December 31.
3. Record the deposit of the repayment of the loan with interest on February 15.

DATE	DESCRIPTION	DR	CR

Question 10

Hoops & Co. generated $500,000 extra cash from the sale of a subsidiary operation. The company treasurer thinks it would be prudent to invest in some bonds as a short-term investment. The company's investment advisor, suggested they use the proceeds to purchase bonds that yield interest of 5% paid annually.

The bonds were purchased for $500,000 on October 1 and sold the following year on June 30 for principal value plus interest. The company has a July 31 year-end.

Required:

Record the journal entries required on October 1 and June 30.

DATE	DESCRIPTION	DR	CR

Question 11

Mailhot Company receives a $1 million government research grant to develop a new product. At the present time, Mailhot is finishing up its previous project, and will not be able to start on its new project for eight months. The controller discovers that some corporate bonds were offering a good interest rate over the short term. The bonds pay 6% interest and were bought on September 1 for $1,020,000 (including $20,000 of accrued interest). Interest is payable semi-annually on October 31 and April 30 each year. Assume Mailhot Company has a June 30th year-end.

Required:

a) Record the purchase of the bonds on September 1.

b) Record the receipts of interest on October 31 and April 30.

DATE	DESCRIPTION	DR	CR

Question 12

XYZ Tools made a large cash sale of power saws and find themselves with unexpected surplus cash of $50,000. With this surplus cash, XYZ purchases stocks and pays a brokerage fee of $250 on September 1. XYZ Tools does not normally purchase investments with surplus cash on a regular basis.

Required: Record the purchase of stocks on September 1.

DATE	DESCRIPTION	DR	CR

Question 13

Tannenbaum Company decides to use its excess cash to take advantage of the recent drop in stock prices. The company has $100,000 of cash and uses part of the cash to purchase 2,000 shares of Goodlett Ltd. On October 7, Tannenbaum paid $47 per share, plus a 1% brokerage fee. Tannenbaum plans to sell the stocks within the next 12 months. Assume the brokerage fee will be capitalized since Tannenbaum Company makes a significant amount of profit by investing excess cash frequently.

Required:

Record the purchase of the stock.

DATE	DESCRIPTION	DR	CR

Question 14

Refer to Question 13. Goodlett Ltd. declares a dividend of $1 per share on September 15, payable to stockholders of record on October 1.

Required:

Prepare the required journal entry for Tannenbaum Company as of October 31.

DATE	DESCRIPTION	DR	CR

Question 15

Refer to Question 13. Assume that on November 30, Tannenbaum sold the stocks for $45 per share.

Required:

Prepare the journal entry required as of November 30.

DATE	DESCRIPTION	DR	CR

Question 16

Refer to Question 13. Assume that on March 31, Tannenbaum Company sold the stocks for $50 per share.

Required:

Prepare the journal entry required as of March 31.

DATE	DESCRIPTION	DR	CR

Question 17

Snelgrove Company purchases 1,000 shares of Kelch Limited on November 7, at a total cost of $40,000. Prior to the purchase date, on October 15, the directors of Kelch Limited declared a dividend of 5 cents per share, payable to stockholders of record on November 9. The dividend will be paid on November 15.

Required:

Prepare the journal entry required on November 15 for Snelgrove Company. Discuss the effect the dividend has on stock price.

DATE	DESCRIPTION	DR	CR

Question 18

Sam's Gardening Tools purchased 100 shares of Green Company for $25 per share on February 1, 2011 for short-term investment purpose. On May 30, Sam's Gardening Tools received dividends of $2 per share.

Required:

a) Record the journal entry for February 1, 2011

b) Record the journal entry for May 30, 2011

c) If Sam's Gardening Tools has a year-end of May 31 and reports income of $45,000 from operations (before any financing income or expense) for the year, what amount of net income will it report after considering the financing activity?

a)

DATE	DESCRIPTION	DR	CR

b)

DATE	DESCRIPTION	DR	CR

c) ______________________________

Question 19

Assume Star Furniture made a big cash sale and would like to invest the extra cash in short-term bonds. On July 1, 2011 (the day the bonds were issued) the company purchases 10, $1,000 short-term bonds. The bonds mature in 6 months on December 31, 2011. The interest rate on the bond is 10%, payable quarterly. A fee of $200 is paid to the broker. Assume Star Furniture has an October 31 year-end. Star Furniture rarely purchases short-term investments.

Required:

a) Record the journal entry on July 1, 2011

b) Record the first interest payment Star Furniture received

c) Record appropriate journal entries on October 31, 2011

a)

DATE	DESCRIPTION	DR	CR

b)

DATE	DESCRIPTION	DR	CR

c)

DATE	DESCRIPTION	DR	CR

Question 20

Refer to the exercise above and assume Star Furniture sold the bonds for $10,500 on December 31, 2011 after receiving the second interest payment. Record all appropriate transactions for December 31, 2011.

DATE	DESCRIPTION	DR	CR

DATE	DESCRIPTION	DR	CR

Question 21

Refer to question 19, assume the brokerage fee is capitalized because Star Furniture trades short-term investment frequently and gains significant income from trading every year.

Required:

a) Record the journal entry on the date of purchase.

b) Assume Star Furniture sold the bonds for a total of $10,000 on December 31, 2011 after receiving the second interest payment. The brokerage fee attached to this transaction is $200. Record the appropriate journal entries.

a)

DATE	DESCRIPTION	DR	CR

b)

DATE	DESCRIPTION	DR	CR

DATE	DESCRIPTION	DR	CR

Question 22

Beta Inc. is a medium size company with a September 30 year-end. From time to time, the company has extra cash on hand which it uses to make short-term investments. During the past year, the company completed the following transactions:

Jan. 1 – Lent $30,000 to another company at an annual rate of 4% and due in 6 months.
Mar. 30 – Purchased 10 Star Company bonds priced at $1,000 each with interest payable semi-annually on September 1 and March 1 at an annual rate of 6%. The company also paid for the amount of accrued interest owing.
Apr.1 – Purchased 500 shares of ABC Company at $60 per share.
July 1 – Received full proceeds from the loan of Jan. 1, including interest.
Sep. 1 – Received 6 months interest payment on the Star Company bonds.
Sep. 1 – Received dividend of $1 per share on the ABC Company stock.
Sep. 30 – Year-end adjustment: record the interest accrued on the Star Company bonds.
Oct. 5 – Sold 200 ABC Company stock for $65 per share.
Dec. 1 – Sold 300 ABC Company stock for $57 per share.

Required:

Record journal entries for each of the above transactions.

DATE	DESCRIPTION	DR	CR

DATE	DESCRIPTION	DR	CR

Case

Your friend, Jami Ringdahl, recently started a new job at Kelly A. Wait Ltd. Jami is responsible for the preparation of the monthly financial statements. Jami commented to you, "The company sure has a lot of cash in the bank!" Since Jami is new to the position and wants to impress her boss, she asks your opinion on the situation. Here are the questions that Jami wants answered:

1. What should the company do with the extra cash?
2. What happens if the company needs the cash for operating activities?
3. How does the above affect the financial statements?
4. Using any values on a journal entry, demonstrate the manner in which cash can be invested in the short-term (include brokerage fees, interest, returns and other costs or gains where applicable).
5. What internal controls are necessary to ensure that the short-term investments are safeguarded?
6. List some potential ethical issues that may arise when investing in the short term.

DATE	DESCRIPTION	DR	CR

DATE	DESCRIPTION	DR	CR

DATE	DESCRIPTION	DR	CR

Critical thinking exercise

1. Discuss the importance to companies of short-term investments, and their effect on the Statement of Financial Position and Statement of Operations.

2. Investing in short-term investments involves deciding which investments to make, investigating possible components, and identifying risks associated with each possible investment. Discuss how you would decide:

    - When to invest in short-term investments

- What you would invest in

- How much risk your company should assume

3. One of the objectives of using short-term investments is to increase income. Are there other ways in which this objective can be accomplished without using short-term investments?

4. Are short-term investments necessary?

5. Are short-term investments wise?

6. Are there other objectives involved in the use of short-term investments?

7. Have companies always used short-term investments?

8. What assumptions are made by a company when it uses short-term investments?

9. Do you think that different countries and cultures have different views regarding short-term investments? Support your answer.

10. What is your personal position on the use of short-term investments?

11. Are they a good idea?

12. Do they expose a company to excess risk?

13. Are there alternatives that can be used to reach the same goal?

14. What is your conclusion on short-term investment and its implications?

15. What is the most important feature of short-term investments?

16. Discuss any other aspects of short-term investments you think are important.

Chapter 7

ACCOUNTS AND NOTES RECEIVABLE

Assessment Questions

Question 1

Define accounts receivable.

Question 2

Describe the presentation of accounts receivable on the balance sheet.

Question 3

What is the crucial record in managing information related to accounts receivable?

Question 4

Explain the relationship between the accounts receivable control account and individual customer accounts in the accounts receivable sub-ledger.

____

____

____

____

Question 5

List the names of the alternative methods for accounting for bad debt. Are both methods allowed under GAAP?

____

____

____

Question 6

Briefly outline the direct write-off method for dealing with bad debt and provide a journal entry example.

____

____

____

____

____

____

DATE	DESCRIPTION	DR	CR

Question 7

Name two different approaches for estimating the bad debt expense when using the AFDA method.

Question 8

Name two ratios used to assess accounts receivable, and state the formulas used to calculate the ratios.

Question 9

What are the risks involved when selling on credit?

Question 10

Which method of accounting for bad debt (direct method or allowance method) is more preferable? Support your answer.

Question 11

If a company uses the allowance method to account for bad debt, which method is best for estimating the allowance: income statement method or balance sheet method?

Question 12

What are the advantages and disadvantages to a company which sells on credit?

Question 13

What pitfalls exist for a company that uses the Income Statement Approach for recording bad debt expense?

Question 14

How do you assess the DSO number? The ART ratio?

Question 15

Give two examples of accounting reports that can be generated involving accounts receivable.

Question 16

What internal controls are important for accounts receivable? Is there any one control that is absolutely necessary?

Question 17

What ethical problems are related to accounts receivable? Can they be avoided?

____

____

____

____

____

____

Application questions

Question 1

On June 15, you discover that your customer, Tyrone Huntzinger, has gone bankrupt. He owes you $1,000. Prepare the appropriate journal entry assuming the direct method is used.

DATE	DESCRIPTION	DR	CR

Question 2

Refer to question 1. Assuming that $5,000 had been credited to the allowance account for the year, prepare the journal entry assuming the allowance method is used.

DATE	DESCRIPTION	DR	CR

Question 3

Your company decides that an allowance for doubtful accounts is required in the amount of $6,000. There is a zero balance in the account. Prepare the journal entry to set up the required allowance.

DATE	DESCRIPTION	DR	CR

Question 4

Your company decides that an allowance for doubtful accounts is required in the amount of $6,000. There is a $4,000 credit balance in the account. Prepare the journal entry to set up the required allowance.

DATE	DESCRIPTION	DR	CR

Question 5

Your company decides that an allowance for doubtful accounts is required in the amount of $6,000. There is a $1,000 debit balance in the account. Prepare the journal entry to set up the required allowance.

DATE	DESCRIPTION	DR	CR

Question 6

A customer's account in the amount of $2,000 was previously written off. Amazingly, on December 31, you receive a check in the mail from the customer with a letter of apology for not paying sooner (the account is 2 years old). Prepare the journal entry by using the allowance method.

DATE	DESCRIPTION	DR	CR

DATE	DESCRIPTION	DR	CR

Question 7

Your company uses the Income Statement Approach for estimating bad debts. Last year, credit sales amounted to $1 million. The estimated bad debts are 0.5% of sales. Prepare the journal entry to record bad debt expense for the year.

DATE	DESCRIPTION	DR	CR

Question 8

Your company uses the balance sheet approach to estimate bad debts. Details of the accounts receivable balances owing are shown below:

Aging Category	Bad debt % (probability of being uncollectible)	Balance	Required allowance
Under 30 days	1%	90,000	900
31-60 days	20%	90,000	18,000
Over 60 days	50%	30,000	15,000
Total		210,000	33,900

Write the journal entry to record bad debt expense for the year, assuming that the allowance account has a $20,000 credit balance.

DATE	DESCRIPTION	DR	CR

Question 9

Wechsler Company has net accounts receivable opening balance of $250,000 and ending balance of $300,000. The total sales amount for the year is $1,700,000. Normal credit terms are 30 days. Calculate the day sales outstanding and the accounts receivable turnover. 80% of the sales are on credit. Comment on the calculated ratios.

Question 10

Lakisha Ogata operates a proprietorship selling machinery. Because of the high value of the machinery sold, Lakisha often requires customers to sign a note. Lakisha originally sold a Gadget machine to Neil Marcin for $10,000 on November 14. The sale was initially recorded as an account receivable, but now Lakisha decides to ask Neil to sign a note. On December 1, Neil signs a one-year note to be paid in quarterly installments, plus 5% interest on the balance outstanding. Lakisha's company has a year end of April 30.

Required:

Prepare an amortization schedule showing the interest and payments due on the note. Use the following format:

Date	Opening balance	Interest	Total	Payment	Closing balance

Prepare the journal entries to reflect the transactions related to the receivable and note.

Date	Opening balance	Interest	Total	Payment	Closing balance

DATE	DESCRIPTION	DR	CR

Question 11

In 2010, Upper Machine Sales Company sold equipment on credit in the amount of $950,000. Total cash collections during the year were $820,000. The company determined that $7,000 of accounts receivable would not be collected and wrote them off. At the end of 2010, management decided to increase its allowance percentage to 1% of credit sales comparing to the 0.5% from last year because of the amount of accounts receivable that proved to be uncollectible during the year. At the end of 2009, the company had $135,000 in Accounts Receivable and a credit balance of $6,000 in Allowance for Doubtful Accounts. Assume the company has a year end of December 31.

Required:

a) Prepare the necessary journal entries to record all 2010 transactions including sales, collection, the write-off, and the new allowance amount. Disregard the dates when recording the transactions.

b) Show the amount of net accounts receivable on the balance sheet as at December 31, 2010.

a)

DATE	DESCRIPTION	DR	CR

b)

____

____

____

Question 12

The 2009 and 2010 sales and accounts receivable information for Velcary Company are shown below:

In 2009, sales for the year totalled $1,200,000 with 60% on credit. At December 31 year end, the accounts receivable had a debit balance of $55,000. The management estimated that 0.5% of all credit sales would be uncollectible. The company wrote off $3,100 worth of accounts receivable at the end of the year.

During the year 2010, sales totalled $1,630,000 with 60% on credit. At the end of 2010, Accounts Receivable has a debit balance of $76,000. Allowance for Doubtful Accounts has a debit balance of $4,500. The bad debt expense for the year have not been determined or recorded. After reviewing the write-offs, the company decided that the estimated percentage for AFDA should be increased from 0.5% to 0.75%.

Required:

a) Prepare the journal entry to record the bad debt expense for 2010.

b) Prepare a T-Account for the Allowance for Doubtful Accounts and enter all related transactions for year 2009 and 2010.

c) What are the net accounts receivable at the end of 2010?

a)

DATE	DESCRIPTION	DR	CR

b)

ALLOWANCE FOR DOUBTFUL ACCOUNTS	

c)

____

____

____

Question 13

Suppose a company has a bonus plan that rewards managers for achieving a certain level of reported net income. What incentives might management have to influence the estimated amount of uncollectible accounts receivable?

____

____

____

____

Question 14

Nortelle Canada operates in an industry that has a high rate of bad debts. Before the year end adjustments, Nortelle Canada's Accounts Receivable has a debit balance of $536,000 and the Allowance for Doubtful Accounts had a credit balance of $20,000. The year-end balance reported on the balance sheet for the Allowance for Doubtful Accounts will be based on the aging schedule shown below:

Aging Category	Bad Debt %	Balance
Less than 16 days	2%	$300,000
16 – 30 days	3%	100,000
31 – 45 days	5%	75,000
46 – 60 days	10%	32,000
61 – 75 days	20%	18,000
Over 75 days	40%	11,000

Required:

a) What is the balance for the Allowance for Doubtful Accounts at year end?

Aging Category	Bad Debt %	Balance	Estimated Amount of Bad Debt
Less than 16 days	2%	$300,000	
16 – 30 days	3%	100,000	
31 – 45 days	5%	75,000	
46 – 60 days	10%	32,000	
61 – 75 days	20%	18,000	
Over 75 days	40%	11,000	

b) Prepare the journal entry to record bad debt expense for the year

DATE	DESCRIPTION	DR	CR

Question 15

A company's relevant accounts receivable information for year 2010 and 2011 is provided below:

	2011	2010
Average Net Accounts Receivable	$1,486,739	$1,769,032
Net Credit Sales	23,075,635	22,107,539

a) Calculate the Accounts Receivable Turnover Ratio for year 2010 and 2011.

b) Calculate the Days Sales Outstanding for year 2010 and 2011.

c) Compare and discuss the results.

Question 15 – answer

a) ______________________________

____

____

____

b) ______________________________

____

____

____

c) ______________________________

____

____

____

Question 16

The following information relevant to accounts receivable is presented for Dommar Company (in thousands of dollars):

	2011	2010	2009
Accounts Receivable	$319	$422	$501
Allowance for Doubtful Accounts	19	18	20
Net Credit Sales	$4,377	$3,598	$2,937

Required:

a) Calculate the Accounts Receivable Turnover Ratio for year 2010 and 2011.

b) Calculate the Day Sales Outstanding for year 2010 and 2011.

c) At the 2010 year end, Dommar Company agreed to sell some of its accounts receivable with a fee paid to the purchaser. Why do you think a company would pay a fee to sell its accounts receivable?

d) Dommar Company sold the accounts receivable on a limited recourse basis. Research and define the meaning of selling on a limited recourse basis.

a) ______________________________

____

____

____

b) ______________________________

____

____

____

c) ______________________________

____

____

____

d) ____

____

____

____

Question 17

On May 1, 2010, People's Networks sold computer networking supplies to Canadian Autos for \$36,000. The cost of the supplies is \$15,000. Instead of paying immediately, Canadian Autos signed a note receivable with 11% annual interest, payable in eight months with the principle amount. People's Networks has a year end of October 31.

Required:

a) Record the journal entry when the sale is made; assume People's Networks uses the perpetual inventory system.

b) Prepare journal entries for the year end adjustment.

c) Prepare journal entries for receipt of payment from Canadian Autos on January 1, 2011.

d) What items would be included on the balance sheet and income statement of People's Networks as at October 31, 2010 with respect to this note?

Question 17 – answer

a)

DATE	DESCRIPTION	DR	CR

b)

DATE	DESCRIPTION	DR	CR

c)

DATE	DESCRIPTION	DR	CR

d)

____

____

____

____

Question 18

On January 1, 2010, Beta Company determined that it would not be able to pay the account receivable that was owed to Star Inc. Beta Company was confident that it would have sufficient cash one year later, therefore signed a one-year note payable for the $10,000 that was owed. The annual interest rate is 9%, payable on July 1 and January 1. Star Inc. has a year end of June 30.

Required:

a) Record journal entries for Star Inc. when the note is signed.

b) Prepare journal entries for the year end adjustment.

c) Prepare journal entries for the receipt of first interest payment.

d) Prepare journal entries for receipt of payment from Beta Company on January 1, 2011.

a)

DATE	DESCRIPTION	DR	CR

b)

DATE	DESCRIPTION	DR	CR

c)

DATE	DESCRIPTION	DR	CR

d)

DATE	DESCRIPTION	DR	CR

Case

You are the Chief Financial Officer for Stanton Feery and Company. Mr. Stanton's friend, Shad Baxtor, is starting up a new company, and needs some advice on accounts receivable and bad debt accounting practices. Mr. Stanton has asked you to meet with Mr. Baxtor, and answer a few questions. He hands you a list of things that Shad Baxtor wants clarified.

Here is the handwritten list:

- What are accounts receivable?
- What are bad debts?
- When are amounts considered bad debts?
- Are there different ways of accounting for bad debt expenses?
- How are bad debts shown on the financial statements?
- Which method is best for accounting for bad debts?
- What kind of reports are important for accounts receivable?
- What is an ageing list?
- What is the difference between a credit sale and a cash sale?
- How can you assess the quality of accounts receivable?
- Should I sell on credit? Are there risks involved?

What are accounts receivable?

What are bad debts?

When are amounts considered bad debts?

Are there different ways of accounting for bad debt expenses?

How are bad debts shown on the financial statements?

Which method is best for accounting for bad debts?

What kind of reports are important for accounts receivable?

What is an aging list?

What is the difference between a credit sale and a cash sale?

How can you assess the quality of accounts receivable?

Should I sell on credit? Are there risks involved?

Chapter 8

INVENTORY

Assessment Questions

Question 1

Explain the difference between a purchase return and a purchase allowance.

Question 2

Explain the difference between a sales allowance and a sales discount.

Question 3

List the different ways of valuing inventory

Question 4

In times of rising prices, which inventory valuation method results in the highest closing inventory? Explain your answer.

Question 5

Different inventory valuation methods result in different inventory values. How should a company select its inventory valuation method?

Question 6

The use of lower of cost or market is based on what GAAP principle?

Question 7

What are the causes of a misstated inventory balance?

Question 8

Name two methods which can be used to estimate inventory for interim statement purposes.

Question 9

Why should a company use a perpetual inventory system?

Question 10

Differentiate the journal entries required for sales when using a perpetual inventory system from the entries required when using a periodic inventory system.

Question 11

List at least three reports that are useful for managing inventory.

Question 12

List at least five internal controls that are useful for controlling and managing inventory.

Application Questions

Question 1

Hip Top Shirt Retailers bought $15,000 worth of shirts from Super Shirt Wholesalers Ltd. on March 15th. Payment was due in April. Prepare the journal entry at the time of purchase. Assume they use the perpetual inventory system.

DATE	DESCRIPTION	DR	CR

Question 2

Referring to the purchase made in Question 1 above, prepare the journal entry for Hip Top Shirt Retailers for the payment of $15,000 made to Super Shirt Wholesalers on April 15th.

DATE	DESCRIPTION	DR	CR

Question 3

Refer to Question 1 above and, assuming Hip Top Shirt uses the *periodic inventory system*, record the journal entries at time of purchase and at time of payment.

DATE	DESCRIPTION	DR	CR

Question 4

JB Supermarkets bought $3,000 worth of groceries on account from a produce supplier on May 10th. On May 11th, JB's bookkeeper was informed that $200 worth of tomatoes was substandard and returned to the supplier. Prepare the journal entry to record the purchase return. Assume they use the perpetual inventory system.

DATE	DESCRIPTION	DR	CR

Question 5

Refer to Question 4 above and record the purchase return assuming JB uses a periodic inventory system.

DATE	DESCRIPTION	DR	CR

Question 6

On January 12th, Corner-Mart received a shipment of T-shirts from Promo Novelties for an event. The invoice amounted to $5,000 and was recorded in the accounting system. Soon after the delivery was made, the marketing manager discovered that the logo was printed incorrectly. The goods were returned to Promo Novelties on January 31st. Prepare the journal entry that would be recorded on January 31st. Assume Corner-Mart uses the perpetual inventory system.

DATE	DESCRIPTION	DR	CR

Question 7

Refer to Question 6 above. Record the purchase return assuming Corner-Mart uses a periodic inventory system.

DATE	DESCRIPTION	DR	CR

Question 8

Signs Unlimited received a shipment of plastic sheets on April 3rd. The value of the plastic was $8,000, plus $100 of freight charges. Prepare the journal entry to record the receipt of goods by Signs Unlimited, assuming the payment would be made in May. Assume they use the perpetual inventory system.

DATE	DESCRIPTION	DR	CR

Question 9

Referring to Question 8 above, several of the plastic sheets delivered to Signs Unlimited were in the wrong colour. After some negotiation, the manager agreed to keep the products with a 10% discount. Prepare the entry on April 10th to record the purchase allowance. (Assume all plastic sheets were still in inventory.) Continue to assume they use the perpetual inventory system.

DATE	DESCRIPTION	DR	CR

Question 10

Refer to Questions 8 and 9 above and journalize the transaction for Signs Unlimited when the payment is made on May 3rd. Continue to assume they use the perpetual inventory system.

DATE	DESCRIPTION	DR	CR

Question 11

Boards Unlimited received a shipment of plastic sheets on April 3rd. The value of the plastic was $8,000, plus $100 of freight charges. Prepare the journal entry to record the receipt of goods by Boards Unlimited, assuming the payment would be made in May. Assume they use the periodic inventory system.

DATE	DESCRIPTION	DR	CR

Question 12

Referring to Question 11 above, several of the plastic sheets delivered to Boards Unlimited were in the wrong colour. After some negotiation, the manager agreed to keep the products with a 10% discount. Prepare the entry on April 10th to record the purchase allowance. (Assume all plastic sheets were still in inventory.) Continue to assume they use the periodic inventory system.

DATE	DESCRIPTION	DR	CR

Question 13

Referring to Questions 11 and 12 above and journalize the transaction for Boards Unlimited when the payment is made on May 3rd. Continue to assume they use the periodic inventory system.

DATE	DESCRIPTION	DR	CR

Question 14

The following is written on an invoice relating to goods that were purchased: 5/10, n/30. What does it mean?

____

____

____

____

Question 15

Shoe Retailers purchased $10,000 worth of shoes from Runner Wear Supplies on March 1st. Since Shoe Retailers has good cash reserves, the accountant took advantage of the early payment discount that Runner Wear offers. Runner Wear's invoice shows terms of 2/10, n/30. What is the latest date that Shoe Retailers could pay the bill to take advantage of the discount?

____

____

Question 16

Refer to Question 15 above. As the bookkeeper for Shoe Retailers, prepare the journal entry to record the purchase on March 1st. Assume they use the perpetual inventory system.

DATE	DESCRIPTION	DR	CR

Question 17

Referring to Question 15 above, journalize the transaction for payment of the invoice, assuming the payment was made on March 5th. Continue to assume they use the perpetual inventory system.

DATE	DESCRIPTION	DR	CR

Question 18

Referring to Question 15 above, journalize the transaction for payment of the invoice, assuming the payment was made on March 30th. Continue to assume they use the perpetual inventory system.

DATE	DESCRIPTION	DR	CR

Question 19

Socks Retailers purchased $10,000 worth of shoes from Jogger Wear Supplies on March 1st. Since Socks Retailers has good cash reserves, the accountant took advantage of the early payment discount that Jogger Wear offers. Jogger Wear's invoice shows terms of 2/10, n/30. What is the latest date that Socks Retailers could pay the bill to take advantage of the discount?

____

____

Question 20

Refer to Question 19 above. As the bookkeeper for Sock Retailers, prepare the journal entry to record the purchase on March 1st. Assume they use the periodic inventory system.

DATE	DESCRIPTION	DR	CR

Question 21

Referring to Question 19 above, journalize the transaction for payment of the invoice, assuming the payment was made on March 5th. Continue to assume they use the periodic inventory system.

DATE	DESCRIPTION	DR	CR

Question 22

Referring to Question 19 above, journalize the transaction for payment of the invoice, assuming the payment was made on March 30th. Continue to assume they use the periodic inventory system.

DATE	DESCRIPTION	DR	CR

Question 23

On March 20th, Cup-A-Java received a shipment of gift mugs for resale from Cup Makers Inc. in the amount of $5,000, plus $200 shipping charges. The terms stated on the invoice from Cup Makers Inc. were as follows: 3/15, n/60. Assume they use the perpetual inventory system. Journalize the following scenarios:

a) As the bookkeeper for Cup-A-Java, complete the original invoice transaction.

DATE	DESCRIPTION	DR	CR

b) If Cup-A-Java decided to take advantage of the early payment cash discount, by when should the payment be made to qualify for the discount?

____

____

c) The payment by Cup-A-Java to Cup Makers Inc. was made on March 31st. prepare the journal entry for the payment of goods. Continue to assume they use the perpetual inventory system.

DATE	DESCRIPTION	DR	CR

d) Journalize the entry if payment was made on May 20th. Continue to assume they use the perpetual inventory system.

DATE	DESCRIPTION	DR	CR

e) On March 25th, 20% of the shipment was returned because they were in the wrong colour. Cup Makers Inc. agreed to apply the same percentage deduction to the freight charges. The invoice has not been paid. Prepare the journal entry to record this transaction. Continue to assume they use the perpetual inventory system.

DATE	DESCRIPTION	DR	CR

f) Continue from (e); journalize the entry if Cup-A-Java took advantage of the early payment cash discount when paying for the balance of the cups on March 31st. round off to the nearest dollar. Continue to assume they use the perpetual inventory system.

DATE	DESCRIPTION	DR	CR

Question 24

If a computer company bought computers for $10,000 and sold them for $14,000, how much would the gross profit be on the entire shipment if the business took advantage of the early cash payment terms of 2/15, n/30 from their supplier?

Question 25

On May 1st, Food Wholesalers purchased $3,000 worth of dried fruit inventory on account and paid $100 for freight charges. On May 15th, Food Wholesalers sold all of the dried fruit inventory to Retail Grocers for $4,000 on account. As the bookkeeper for Food Wholesalers, journalize the transactions. Assume they use the perpetual inventory system.

DATE	DESCRIPTION	DR	CR

Question 26

Referring to Question 25 above, if operating expenses were $500:

a) How much was Food Wholesalers' gross profit?

____

____

b) How much was Food Wholesalers' net profit?

____

____

Question 27

Macks is a maker of cotton garments that sells to various retailers. On June 1st, Cory's Retailers sent back a shipment of goods that was unsatisfactory. As a gesture of good will, Macks agreed to the return of the goods. The goods were sold on account for $6,000 originally and cost $4,000. Assume they use the perpetual inventory system. Complete the following:

a) As Mack's bookkeeper prepare the journal entries to reflect the return.

DATE	DESCRIPTION	DR	CR

b) Journalize the entry if Cory's only returned half of the shipment. Continue to assume they use the perpetual inventory system.

DATE	DESCRIPTION	DR	CR

c) What happened to the value of Macks' owner's equity when Cory's returned the merchandise? Did it increase, decrease or stay the same? Explain your answer.

____

____

____

d) Explain the logic behind debiting the sales returns and allowances as a contra-account instead of debiting the revenue account directly.

____

____

____

____

____

____

Question 28

Assume you are the bookkeeper for Moira's Wholesalers, a distributor of kitchen furniture. Your sales manager informed you that Ted's Retailers were unhappy with the quality of some tables delivered on August 12th, and they will be shipping back all the goods. The original invoice amounted to $1,500 and the goods cost Moira's $1,000. Assume they use the perpetual inventory system. Complete the journal entries for each of the following scenarios:

a) Rather than taking the tables back, your sales manager agreed to allow Ted's Retailers a 10% discount if they agreed to keep the goods. Record Ted's payment in settlement of the invoice on September 12th.

DATE	DESCRIPTION	DR	CR

b) Suppose that Ted's shipped back all the goods on August 15th. Journalize the transactions. Continue to assume they use the perpetual inventory system.

DATE	DESCRIPTION	DR	CR

c) Suppose that Ted's shipped back half the goods on August 15th and kept the other half with 10% discount. Journalize the transactions that took place on August 15th. Continue to assume they use the perpetual inventory system.

DATE	DESCRIPTION	DR	CR

d) Continue from question 28(b). Since all the goods were sold and returned in the same period, what happened to Moira's gross profit? (Disregard the additional shipping and administration costs). Explain your answer.

Question 29

Pete's Wholesalers imports and distributes towels. They sell their products to various retailers throughout the country and offer payments terms of 2/10, n/30. On October 1st, Pete's made a large sale to Ernie's Bathroom Retailers in the amount of $15,000, which cost Pete's $9,000. Pete's uses a perpetual inventory system. Complete the following:

a) Journalize the sale that was made on account.

DATE	DESCRIPTION	DR	CR

b) By what date must Ernie's pay the invoice to qualify for the early cash payment discount?

c) Assume Ernie's paid the bill on October 5th. Record the journal entries. Continue to assume they use the perpetual inventory system.

DATE	DESCRIPTION	DR	CR

d) If Ernie's had returned half the shipment and paid for the balance owing on October 5th, how would the transaction be journalized? Continue to assume they use the perpetual inventory system.

DATE	DESCRIPTION	DR	CR

e) Suppose Ernie's found the goods unsatisfactory and agreed to keep the goods with a 10% discount. Prepare the journal entry to record the sales allowance and Ernie's payment on October 20th. Continue to assume they use the perpetual inventory system.

DATE	DESCRIPTION	DR	CR

f) Referring to scenario 29(a) - Ernie's kept the entire shipment and paid the invoice on October 10th to take advantage of the early payment discount. Record the journal entries for the payment to Pete's. Continue to assume they use the perpetual inventory system.

DATE	DESCRIPTION	DR	CR

Question 30

Assume you are the bookkeeper for Joe The Printer. The company buys ink cartridges from various suppliers, refills them and sells them to customers. All purchases and sales are made on account. Assume they use the perpetual inventory system. Complete the following for Joe The Printer.

a) Record the purchase on December 15th of $3,000 ink cartridges from Inkster Supplies, whose payment terms are 3/10, n/45.

DATE	DESCRIPTION	DR	CR

b) When must Joe's pay the account to qualify for the discount?

____

____

c) Prepare the journal entry to record Joe's payment on December 20th. Continue to assume they use the perpetual inventory system.

DATE	DESCRIPTION	DR	CR

d) If Joe's made the payment on December 31st instead, journalize the transaction. Continue to assume they use the perpetual inventory system.

DATE	DESCRIPTION	DR	CR

e) If Joe's returned 1/3rd of the products and paid the balance, how would both of these transactions be journalized? Assume both transactions occurred on December 20th. Continue to assume they use the perpetual inventory system.

DATE	DESCRIPTION	DR	CR

f) If on January 5th, Joe's sold all $3,000 worth of inventory for $5,000 to Smith printers on account, how would the transactions be journalized? Continue to assume they use the perpetual inventory system.

DATE	DESCRIPTION	DR	CR

g) Continue from the previous question. If Joe's selling terms were 4/7, n/30, prepare the journal entry to record receipt of payment on January 12th. Continue to assume they use the perpetual inventory system.

DATE	DESCRIPTION	DR	CR

Question 31

Fill in the missing numbers on the perpetual inventory record. The company uses the weighted average cost for inventory.

Inventory Sub Ledger Account					
		Purchase / Sales		Quantity on Hand	
Date	**Description**	**Quantity**	**Amount**	**Quantity**	**Amount**
	Purchase from AAA Co.	200	$2,000	?	?
	Sale to SSS Co.	?	?	100	1,000
	Sale to TTT Co.	-50	?	50	500
	Purchase from BBB	60	720	?	?
	Sale to UUU Co.	-20	?	90	?

Question 32

Use the information from your completed answer to Question 31. What is the cost of each unit sold to UUU Co. using the FIFO method?

Question 33

Use the information from your completed answer to Question 31. What is the total cost of the units sold to UUU Co. using Specific Identification? 10 of the units sold to UUU were purchased from AAA, and 10 units were purchased from BBB.

Question 34

Complete the following table, based on the information in your completed Question 31.

	Specific Identification	Average Cost	FIFO
Balance Before Sale to UUU			
COGS on Sale to UUU			
Closing inventory Balance			

Question 35

A company has three types of products: gadgets, widgets and gizmos. The cost of each type is listed below. Complete the table by applying the lower of cost or market method.

				Lower of Cost or Market Applied to...		
Description	**Category**	**Cost**	**Market**	**Individual**	**Category**	**Total**
Gadget Type 1	Gadgets	$1,000	$900	?		
Gadget Type 2	Gadgets	5,000	5,200	?		
Total Gadgets		?	?		?	
Widget A	Widgets	100	100	?		
Widget B	Widgets	20	200	?		
Total Widgets		?	?		?	
Gizmo 1	Gizmos	1,500	1,450	?		
Gizmo 2	Gizmos	1,750	2,000	?		
Total Gizmos		?	?		?	
Total		?	?	?	?	?

Question 36

A company reported ending inventory of $100,000 in year 1. It was discovered in year 2 that the correct value of the ending inventory was $90,000 for year 1. Complete the following table, based on this information. Assume the company uses perpetual inventory.

Item	Reported	Correct Amount
Inventory	$100,000	
Current Assets	$150,000	
Total Assets	$500,000	
Owner's Equity year 1	$200,000	
Owner's Equity year 2	$235,000	
Sales	$1,000,000	
Cost of Goods Sold	$500,000	
Profit for year 1	$6,000	
Profit for year 2	$15,000	

Question 37

Assume that you have to prepare quarterly financial statements, and the following information is available from the General Ledger:

Sales	$200,000
Opening Inventory	$67,000
Purchases	$90,000
Gross Profit Margin (from examination of prior years' statements) = 30%	

Required:

Calculate the estimated closing inventory using the gross profit method.

Question 38

Shown below is the current information for a company.

	At Cost	At Retail
Cost of Goods Sold		
Opening Inventory	2,000	4,000
Purchases	42,000	90,000
Cost of Goods Available for Sale	44,000	94,000
Sales at Retail		50,000
Closing Inventory at Retail		44,000

Required:

Calculate the estimated closing inventory at cost by using the retail method.

Question 39

A company purchases 1,000 units of inventory at $12 per unit on account. The company subsequently sells 25 units for $50 per unit on account. The company uses a perpetual inventory system.

Required:

a) Write the journal entries that record the above transactions.

b) Write the journal entries as if the company used a periodic inventory system.

DATE	DESCRIPTION	DR	CR

Question 40

The following is a list of relevant inventory numbers from ABC Company for the 2010 fiscal year:

	$ Millions
Inventory - December 31, 2009	$108.5
Inventory - December 31, 2010	169.7
Cost of Goods Sold	$1,452.5

A list of relevant inventory numbers from XYZ Company for the 2010 fiscal year:

	$ Millions
Inventory - December 31, 2009	$221.7
Inventory - December 31, 2010	209.6
Cost of Goods Sold	$1,432.0

Required:

a) Calculate the Inventory Turnover Ratio and Inventory Days on Hand for ABC Company.

b) Calculate the Inventory Turnover Ratio and Inventory Days on Hand for XYZ Company.

c) Compare the results between two companies. What conclusion can we draw about the performance of these two companies comparatively?

Question 41

Delta Corporation reported the following amounts for ending inventory and cost of goods sold in the financial statements:

Ending Inventory	
2011	$799,000
2010	$1,365,000
2009	$3,205,000

Cost of Goods Sold	
2011	$25,927,000
2010	$36,479,000
2009	$47,025,000

Required:

a) Calculate the Inventory Turnover Ratio and Inventory Days on Hand for the year 2011 and 2010.

b) Compare and discuss the results between two years.

c) Delta Corporation is a software company in a rapidly changing industry. Evaluate the results from part (a) by using this information and considering the amount of cost of goods sold.

Question 42

Simplex Inc. has a fiscal year end on December 31. Below is an inventory purchase and sales record for the year 2011. The company has only one product in inventory, and all units of that product are identical (homogenous).

Date	Units Purchased	Units Sold	Units Balance
January 1			15 @ $10 each
February 13	20 @$12 each		
March 26	15 @ 13 each		
April 17		40 @ $20 each	
July 25	50 @$14 each		
September 28		35 @ $20 each	
November 3		20 @ $20 each	
December 31			5

Required:

a) Assume that Simplex Inc. uses the periodic inventory system and valuates inventory by using the weighted average method. Calculate the value of ending inventory at December 31.

b) Assume that Simplex Inc. uses the perpetual inventory system and valuates inventory by using the First-In-First-Out (FIFO) method. Calculate the value of cost of goods sold (COGS) for the year.

Question 43

Refer to question 42 and answer the following:

a) Assume that Simplex Inc. uses the periodic inventory system and valuates inventory using the First-In-First-Out (FIFO) method during 2011. Prepare journal entries for recognizing the sale of 40 units at $20 per unit (recognizing COGS if applicable) on April 17. Assume that the sale is made on account. For each component of the journal entries, clearly state whether the debit/credit is made to an income statement (I/S) account or a balance sheet (B/S) account. (For example, Dr. Cash (B/S) $10; Cr. Revenue (I/S) $10)

b) Assume that Simplex Inc. uses the perpetual inventory system and valuates inventory using the First-In-First-Out (FIFO) method during 2011. Prepare journal entries for recognizing the sale of 35 units at $20 per unit (recognizing COGS if applicable) on September 28. Assume that the sale is made on account. For each component of the journal entries, clearly state whether the debit/credit is made to an income statement (I/S) account or a balance sheet (B/S) account. (For example, Dr. Cash (B/S) $10; Cr. Revenue (I/S) $10)

a)

DATE	DESCRIPTION	DR	CR

b)

DATE	DESCRIPTION	DR	CR

Question 44

Garden Inc. uses the periodic inventory system and its inventory consists of four products as at December 31, 2011. Selected information is provided below:

Product	Number of units	Cost (per unit)	Expected selling price (per unit)
1	15	$80	$120
2	20	$80	$60
3	40	$60	$50
4	5	$120	$180

Required:

Calculate the inventory value that should be reported on December 31, 2011, using the lower of cost or market approach applied on an individual-item basis.

Product	Number of units	Cost (per unit)	Expected selling price (per unit)	LCM (Individual)
1	15	$80	$120	
2	20	$80	$60	
3	40	$60	$50	
4	5	$120	$180	

____

____

Question 45

Refer to question 44. It is now March 31, 2012 and Garden Inc.needs to present a set of financial statements showing the performance of the first quarter of 2012 to a local bank for a loan. To prepare the statements in a timely manner, Garden Inc. decided to estimate the inventory amount instead of doing a physical count. The following information is provided:

Accounts Receivable, January 1, 2012	$1,500
Accounts Receivable, March 31, 2012	2,200
Collections of accounts from January 1 to March 31	5,300
Inventory, January 1, 2012	1,200
Purchases from January 1 to March 31	6,800

Assume all sales are made on account. The sale prices of the products are determined by marking up costs by 25%.

Required:

Calculate the estimated cost of the inventory on March 31, 2012 using the gross profit method.

Question 46

Good Life Corporation sells medical support products and records purchases at net amounts. They account for their inventory using the periodic system. In 2011, the following information was available from the company's inventory records for ankle support products.
A physical count was taken on March 31, 2011 and showed 2,000 units on hand.

	Units	Unit Cost
January 1, 2011 (beginning inventory)	1,600	$18.00
Purchases		
January 5, 2011	2,600	$20.00
January 25, 2011	2,400	$21.00
February 16, 2011	1,000	$22.00
March 15, 2011	1,800	$23.00

Required:

a) Prepare schedules to calculate the ending inventory at March 31, 2011 under the FIFO valuation method.

b) Prepare schedules to calculate the ending inventory at March 31, 2011 under the weighted average valuation method.

c) Explain why the LIFO method may be a poor way to value inventory.

a)

b)

c)

Case

1. Record the following for a company using a perpetual inventory system (using FIFO).

The company has no widgets in its opening inventory.

a) Purchase of 1,000 widgets at $20 each on credit
b) Sale of 900 widgets at $55 each for cash
c) Purchase of 500 widgets at $25 each on credit
d) Sale of 100 widgets at $60 on credit
e) Sale of 300 widgets at $50 each for cash

2. Prepare the perpetual inventory record for the preceding transactions. The company uses FIFO inventory methods.
3. Prepare a statement showing Sales, Cost of Sales and Gross profit.
4. The company physically counted and valued the inventory, and prepared the following table. Complete the table using individual item LCM methods.
5. The company physically counted the inventory and found out that there was an inventory shrinkage of $300. Record the adjusting entry required.
6. Sales for the following interim period are $100,000 and purchases were $68,500. Calculate the gross profit margin and prepare an interim statement for the period, using the gross profit method to estimate inventory. (Use the information from your previous answers)

1.

DATE	DESCRIPTION	DR	CR

2.

Inventory Sub Ledger Account					
		Purchase / Sales		Quantity on Hand	
Date	Description	Quantity	Amount	Quantity	Amount

3.

4.

				Lower of Cost or Market Applied to...		
Description	**Category**	**Cost**	**Market**	**Individual**	**Category**	**Total**
Widget A	Widgets	3,000	2,700			
Widget B	Widgets	2,000	3,300			
Total Widgets		5,000	6,000			
TOTAL		**5,000**	**6,000**			

5.

DATE	DESCRIPTION	DR	CR

6.

Critical Thinking Exercise

1. Lower of cost and market may be calculated using one of three methods. Which method is best? Support your answer.
2. Inventory can be estimated using the gross profit method or the retail method. Counting and valuing inventory can be an expensive process (labour cost, closing retail stores while count is underway, etc.) Is it necessary to count and value inventory when it can be estimated? Explain your answer.
3. Profits can be easily manipulated by management by misstating the amount of inventory. Discuss the methods by which management can report incorrect inventory amounts, and the means by which such errors can be eliminated, or at least, reduced.

Notes

Chapter 9

PREPAID EXPENSES AND OTHER CURRENT ASSETS

Assessment Questions

Question 1

List *at least* five examples of prepaid expenses.

Question 2

Over time, the asset-prepaid expenses converts to what account?

Question 3

Which assets are classified as miscellaneous current assets?

Question 4

Give an example of a miscellaneous current asset.

Question 5

According to the General Index of Financial Reporting, which of the following items could be classified as other current assets?

1. accounts receivable
2. accrued investment income
3. cash
4. drilling advances
5. future income taxes
6. security deposits
7. taxes recoverable

Question 6

List the characteristics of prepaid assets and other current assets.

____

____

____

____

____

____

Question 7

What is the primary objective of internal controls related to prepaid expenses and other current assets?

____

____

____

____

____

Question 8

A company pays $5,000 rent on the first day of the month for the current month. Should the amount be classified as a prepaid expense? Discuss.

____

____

____

____

____

____

Question 9

A company pays for insurance at the beginning of its fiscal year, and charges the amount to insurance expense. Is this procedure correct? Discuss.

Question 10

You paid $600 in advance for 12 months worth of internet service. After three months, you find a better deal, and advise your current internet supplier. According to your contract, you may cancel at any time. When you paid for the service, the amount was charged to prepaid expenses. What amount should the refund be? What is the correct journal entry to record the refund?

Application Questions

Question 1

A company paid $12,000 cash for 12 months worth of insurance on March 1. The company's fiscal year ends on January 31. Prepare the journal entry to record the payment.

DATE	DESCRIPTION	DR	CR

Question 2

A company paid $12,000 cash for 12 months worth of insurance on March 1, 20x1, and debited the total amount to prepaid insurance. The company's fiscal year ends on January 31. Prepare the journal entry required on January 31, 20x2, assuming no other entries affecting prepaid insurance have been made. If the amount was paid on Mar. 1, there would be 1 month of prepaid expense left in the asset account for February.

DATE	DESCRIPTION	DR	CR

Question 3

Use the data from Question 1. Prepare the journal entry required on January 31, assuming that instead of debiting prepaid insurance, the accountant debited insurance expense for the amount of $12,000 on March 1st when the insurance was paid.

DATE	DESCRIPTION	DR	CR

Question 4

Use the data from Question 1. Assume that an entry has been made each month during the year. Prepare the journal entry required on January 31.

DATE	DESCRIPTION	DR	CR

Question 5

Refer to question 4. What would be the balance in the insurance expense account and the prepaid insurance account after recording the January journal entry?

____

____

____

____

____

Question 6

Extreme Cruise Inc. is a travel agency with a year-end of August 31. During the 2010 fiscal year, the following transactions occurred:

- January 1 – paid cash for yearly insurance premium of $2,400
- July 1 – paid $4,500 cash for 3-month rent in advance

Required:

a) Record the purchase of prepaid insurance on January 1.

b) Recognize 8 months of prepaid insurance as an expense on August 31.

c) Record the rent prepayment on July 1.

d) Recognize 2 months of prepaid rent as an expense on August 31.

a)

DATE	DESCRIPTION	DR	CR

b)

DATE	DESCRIPTION	DR	CR

c)

DATE	DESCRIPTION	DR	CR

d)

DATE	DESCRIPTION	DR	CR

Question 7

Refer to question 6 and answer the following:

a) What would be the balances of the insurance expense and prepaid insurance accounts on August 31?

b) What would be the balances of the rent expense and prepaid rent accounts on August 31?

c) How would recognizing prepaid expense affect equity?

Question 8

Part of the trial balance for Greg's Cottage Ltd. On June 30, 2011 is shown below:

Account Title	Debit	Credit
Cash	$19,600	
Prepaid Insurance	4,500	
Office Supplies	2,600	

Additional Information:

i) The balance in prepaid insurance is a one year premium paid on April 1, 2011.

ii) A physical count shows $450 of office supplies are still on hand.

Required:

a) Journalize the adjustment for prepaid insurance as at June 30, 2011.

b) Journalize the adjustment for office supplies as at June 30, 2011.

c) Prepare the adjusted amounts for the three accounts provided.

a)

DATE	DESCRIPTION	DR	CR

b)

DATE	DESCRIPTION	DR	CR

c)

Account Title	Debit	Credit
Cash		
Prepaid Insurance		
Office Supplies		

Question 9

Selected accounts from a partial adjusted trial balance of Alpha Inc. at January 31, 2011 is shown below (assume the accounting period begins on January 1):

Account Title	Debit	Credit
Cash	$15,000	
Prepaid Insurance	2,400	
Office Supplies	700	
Supplies Expense	950	
Insurance Expense	400	

Required:

a) If the amount in Supplies Expense is the January 31 adjusting entry, and $600 supplies were purchased in January, what was the beginning balance in Supplies on January 1?

b) If the amount in Insurance Expense is the January 31 adjusting entry, and the original insurance premium was for one year, what was the total premium and when was the policy purchased?

Question 10

One of the examples of prepaid expenses could be the tuition you pay. Assume that one semester's tuition costs $2,500 and you make a single payment at the beginning of the semester.

Required:

Prepare the tuition transaction at the beginning of the semester and at the end of the semester on your own books.

At the beginning of the semester:

DATE	DESCRIPTION	DR	CR

At the end of the semester:

DATE	DESCRIPTION	DR	CR

Question 11

You are the new junior accountant for Acme Printing Company. Your fiscal year ends on December 31. You are responsible for preparing monthly financial statements. Acme Printing Company estimated its property tax bill for 2011 to be $12,000.

During February 2011, Acme received the actual property tax bill for 2009 in the amount of $15,300. Each installment is to be paid on the following dates:

Feb 28	$4,300
May 1	4,000
Jul 1	4,000
Sep 1	3,000

Assume the January 31, 2011 adjusting entries and financial statements have already been prepared and that the following journal entry was recorded:

DATE	DESCRIPTION	DR	CR
Jan 31	Property Tax Expense	1,000	
	Property Tax Payable		1,000
	To record 1 month of property tax expense ($12,000/12 = $1,000) based on estimate for the year		

Step 1. What is the amount that will be allocated as property tax expense for each month, starting from February? Note that the expense for January has already been allocated but Property Expense for the year is now known to be $15,300 rather than $12,000.

____

____

____

____

____

Step 2. Record the journal entries for the monthly adjusting entries to record property tax expense for 2011 plus the 4 installment payments listed above.

DATE	DESCRIPTION	DR	CR

Prepaid Property Tax

DATE	DESCRIPTION	DR	CR

Prepaid Property Tax

Prepaid Property Tax

Prepaid Property Tax

Prepaid Property Tax

Prepaid Property Tax

Prepaid Property Tax

Prepaid Property Tax

DATE	DESCRIPTION	DR	CR

Prepaid Property Tax

Prepaid Property Tax

Prepaid Property Tax

Prepaid Property Tax

Prepaid Property Tax

Prepaid Property Tax

Case

Select a company for this exercise. The company must have more than $1 billion in capitalization. You can check out the capitalization of the company by going to the globeinvestor.com website, and using the filter (see below).

Go to the Sedar.com website, and examine the financial statements of the company using the most recent annual report. Include applicable sections of the company financial statements in your report. Prepare a report showing the following:

- Name of company
- Year-end
- Market capitalization
- The industry in which the company operates
- Amount of prepaid and other assets (note: the company must report prepaid expenses and/or other assets)
- Amount of total current assets
- Amount of total assets
- Prepaid as a percentage of current assets
- Prepaid as a percentage of total assets
- Makeup of prepaid and other current assets (if any); this information is usually found in the notes to the financial statements.

What are your thoughts on prepaid assets (as compared to current and total assets)? Compare your information with at least one other student report.

Critical Thinking Exercise

Relatively speaking, prepaid expenses and other assets are immaterial with respect to other assets on the balance sheet. Is it always necessary to disclose these assets, or should they be combined with other assets? Discuss.

Chapter 10

LONG-TERM ASSETS

Assessment Questions

Question 1

Where would one expect to find capital assets listed on the statement of financial position (Balance Sheet)?

Question 2

Define Capital Assets. Give an example of a capital asset.

Question 3

When deciding whether or not to classify an amount as a capital asset, what criteria are used?

Question 4

What is meant by a lump sum purchase of assets? How are costs allocated when the purchase of assets is a lump sum purchase?

Question 5

After the initial purchase of a capital asset, additional costs may be incurred. What criteria are used to assess whether this cost is regarded as an expense or an addition to assets?

Question 6

What is the residual value of an asset? By what other name is residual value known?

Question 7

Name three different methods of calculating depreciation.

Question 8

Does a company always receive the estimated salvage value of an asset on disposal? Assuming the asset is fully depreciated, how is the difference between the estimated and actual salvage value treated?

Question 9

What does the net book value of a capital asset represent? Does the net book value represent the market value of the asset?

Question 10

List five different methods of dealing with partial-year depreciation.

Question 11

In which section of the balance sheet are intangible assets found?

Question 12

Discuss the differences between intangible assets and other fixed assets (i.e. Property, Plant and Equipment).

Question 13

Define intangible assets and describe the costs that are included in calculating its value.

Question 14

Define goodwill.

Question 15

How do you calculate the value of goodwill?

Question 16

What is the major difference between goodwill and other intangible assets?

Question 17

What method is usually used to record the depletion of natural resources?

Question 18

How is per unit amortization calculated?

Question 19

List three examples of intangible assets.

Question 20

What alternative is available for companies that do not want to own fixed tangible assets?

Application Questions

Question 1

Prepare the journal entry for the purchase of a capital asset worth $200,000 (on credit).

DATE	DESCRIPTION	DR	CR

Question 2

Land, building and equipment were purchased for a total amount of $1.5 million. The assessed values of these purchases were, Land - $0.9 MM; Building - $0.5 MM; Equipment – $0.2 MM. Write the journal entry that records the purchase. Round your figures to two decimal points.

Item	Assessment	Percent	Applied to Cost
Land			
Building			
Equipment			
Total			

DATE	DESCRIPTION	DR	CR

Question 3

Prepare the journal entry to record depreciation of $2,000 for a capital asset.

DATE	DESCRIPTION	DR	CR

Question 4

An asset was purchased at the beginning of the year for $50,000. The asset is expected to last for four years, at which time the estimated residual value will be $10,000. Prepare a table showing the year, the cost of the asset, the amount of depreciation expense each year, accumulated depreciation to date, and net book value. The company uses straight-line depreciation.

Year	Cost of Capital Asset	Depreciation Expense	Accumulated Depreciation To Date	Net Book Value

Question 5

Refer to the data supplied in question 4. The asset was sold for $12,000 cash on the first day of year 5. Prepare the journal entry to record the sale.

DATE	DESCRIPTION	DR	CR

Question 6

Use the data supplied in question 4. Prepare the table assuming that the company used double-declining-balance depreciation and the asset had no residual value.

Year	Net Book Value at the Beginning of the Year	Depreciation Expense	Accumulated Depreciation To Date	Net Book Value at the End of the Year

Question 7

Use the data supplied in question 4. Assume that the company uses the units-of production method. The asset can produce 1 million units. Record of production: year 1 – 300,000 units; year 2 – 250,000; year 3 – 300,000 units; year 4 – 100,000 units. Prepare a table showing the year, the cost of the asset, the amount of depreciation expense each year, accumulated depreciation to date, and net book value. Hint: depreciate the cost of the asset minus its residual value.

Year	Cost of Capital Asset	Depreciation Expense	Accumulated Depreciation To Date	Net Book Value

Question 8

On June 15, 2000, Bob's Juice Factory purchased a new bottle-sealing machine for $102,000. The machine had an estimated useful life of 10 years and is expected to have no residual value. Assume that the company has adopted a partial-year depreciation policy, where no depreciation is taken in the year of the purchase, and yearly depreciation thereafter, including the year of disposal. Prepare the table using these facts. The company uses straight-line depreciation. The asset is sold on November 1, 2008 for $35,000. The fiscal year-end for Bob's Juice Factory is December 31. Record the entry for the sale.

Year	Cost of Capital Asset	Depreciation Expense	Accumulated Depreciation To Date	Net Book Value

DATE	DESCRIPTION	DR	CR

Question 9

At the beginning of Year 1, an entrepreneur purchased a group of assets as a "bulk purchase" at an auction sale. The entrepreneur paid $250,000 "as is" for 2 automobiles, a widget machine, a forklift truck, and a trailer. The items were valued by a professional appraiser as follows:

Item	Estimated Value	Percentage	Estimated Remaining Life
Auto 1	$10,000	3.22%	3 Years
Auto 2	15,000	4.83%	5 Years
Widget Machine	258,000	83.23%	15 Years
Fork-lift	15,000	4.83%	5 Years
Trailer	12,000	3.87%	10 Years
Total	$310,000	100%	

After the auction, the entrepreneur had the machine moved to the factory. Moving the widget machine cost $2,000. After the machine was placed in the factory, an electrician was contracted to install additional power lines and hook up the machine at a cost of $1,000. A plumber was also needed to connect the machine to the water mains. This cost $500. A gas fitter was required to connect the widget machine to the gas line at a cost of $200.

Before placing Auto 1 and 2 into use, the entrepreneur took both autos to the local repair shop. The mechanic said that Auto 1 needed a new engine that would cost $2,000 and Auto

2 needed a major tune-up at a cost of $500 (the tune-up is required to get the car going). The entrepreneur paid cash for the repairs. Early on in Year 2, the entrepreneur advertised and sold Auto 1 for $8,000 and replaced the front brakes on Auto 2 for $300.

The entrepreneur's company uses a half-year method for depreciation (i.e. ½ year's depreciation in the year of purchase, and ½ year's depreciation in the year of sale). No depreciation is recorded if an item is bought and sold in the same year. The company uses straight-line depreciation, with an estimated residual value of 10% of cost for all assets.

Required:

Write the journal entries to record the following:

1. Using straight-line depreciation method, record all journal entries related to the above transactions. Hint: when allocating a bulk purchase, round up to the nearest dollar. If the numbers don't quite balance because of rounding, adjust the largest number up or down so that the journal entry balances.
2. Using the double-declining-balance depreciation method, redo the journal entries for the depreciation of the Trailer for years 1 and 2.

1.

DATE	DESCRIPTION	DR	CR

DATE	DESCRIPTION	DR	CR

2.

DATE	DESCRIPTION	DR	CR

Calculations

	Bulk Purchase	Tune Up	Book Value	Residual 10%	Less Residual	Yrs	Less Residual Div by Yrs	Half Yr Method	Round
Auto 1 Year 1									
Auto 1 Year 2									
Auto 2*									
Widget									
Fork Lift									
Trailer									
*Note $300 for brakes classed as maintenance, not capital Note $500 for tune needed to get the car going is capital									

Question 10

Two years ago, an asset was purchased for $50,000. The asset was expected to last for four years (with an estimated residual value of $10,000). For the first two years, the company used the double declining balance (as in Question 6). Suppose the company decides to switch to the straight–line method after recording the depreciation expense for year 2. Calculate the depreciation expense for year 3.

Question 11

Use the data supplied in question 10. Assume that the company has adopted a partial-year depreciation policy, wherein ½ a year's depreciation is taken in the year of purchase, and ½ a year's depreciation is recorded in the year of disposal and that the asset is sold at the beginning of Year 3 for $20,000. Prepare the table and journal entry required to record the sale using these facts. The company uses straight-line depreciation.

Year	Cost of Capital Asset	Depreciation Expense	Accumulated Depreciation To Date	Net Book Value

DATE	DESCRIPTION	DR	CR

Question 12

John Partington purchased the assets ($500,000) and liabilities ($400,000) of a company for which he paid $150,000. The company owns the rights to a unique product. Record the purchase transaction.

DATE	DESCRIPTION	DR	CR

Question 13

Refer to question 12. Subsequent to the purchase of the company, a competitor appeared. John assessed that the value of the goodwill, which his company owned, was now worth $20,000. Record the appropriate journal entry to reflect the reduction in the value of goodwill.

DATE	DESCRIPTION	DR	CR

Question 14

Turpen Corporation purchased timber rights from the government. The License lasts for 10 years, during which time Turpen estimates that 10 million BF of lumber can be harvested. The company paid $10,000,000 for the License. The license has zero value on expiry. Record the journal entry for the purchase of the timber rights.

DATE	DESCRIPTION	DR	CR

Question 15

Refer to question 14 above. Calculate the Unit Price for each BF to be extracted.

___

___

Question 16

Refer to questions 14 and 15. During the current year, the company harvested 500,000 BF. Record the journal entry to record the harvesting.

DATE	DESCRIPTION	DR	CR

Question 17

Feggins Company purchased a patent from Marquette Limited for $200,000. The patent has a remaining life of six years. Prepare the journal entry to record the purchase.

DATE	DESCRIPTION	DR	CR

Question 18

Refer to question 17. Prepare the journal entry to record amortization for one year. The company does not use the half-year rule.

DATE	DESCRIPTION	DR	CR

Question 19

Mirabella Manufacturing spent several years developing a process for producing widgets. Their lawyer suggested that they patent the process. Accordingly, the company proceeded to obtain the patent. In order to patent the process, the company paid $100,000 to the lawyer, plus $25,000 to the government for the patent. In addition, other fees incurred relating to the patent of $10,000. Prepare the journal entries to record the cost of the patent.

DATE	DESCRIPTION	DR	CR

Question 20

Refer to question 19. The patent has a life of 17 years. Prepare the journal entry to amortize the patent for one year.

DATE	DESCRIPTION	DR	CR

Case 1

Canadian National Railway and Canadian Pacific Railway are two companies in the same industry. Obtain copies of their most recent financial statements (at www.sedar.com), locate the capital assets on the statement of financial position, and read the notes to the financial statements that cover capital assets.

1. What is the amount of net assets for each company?
2. What method does each company use to calculate depreciation?
3. What rate does each company use for depreciation?
4. Assume that each company added $1 million of rails. What is the amount of depreciation for one year. (Hint – assume that the rails are in first position. Use the average estimated years of service life for CP).

5. Why do you think CN and CP use different rates of depreciation?

Item	CNR	CP
Net Assets		
Method		
Rate		
Depreciation on $1MM		

	2007	*2006*
Properties *(Note 5)*	20,413	21,053

Note 1 to financial statements

G. Properties

Railroad properties are carried at cost less accumulated depreciation including asset impairment write-downs. Labor, materials and other costs associated with the installation of rail, ties, ballast and other track improvements are capitalized to the extent they meet the Company's minimum threshold for capitalization. Major overhauls and large refurbishments are also capitalized when they result in an extension to the useful life or increase the functionality of the asset. Included in property additions are the costs of developing computer software for internal use. Maintenance costs are expensed as incurred.

The cost of railroad properties, less net salvage value, retired or disposed of in the normal course of business is charged to accumulated depreciation, in accordance with the group method of depreciation. The Company reviews the carrying amounts of properties held and used whenever events or changes in circumstances indicate that such carrying amounts may not be recoverable based on future undiscounted cash flows. Assets that are deemed impaired as a result of such review are recorded at the lower of carrying amount or fair value.

Assets held for sale are measured at the lower of their carrying amount or fair value, less cost to sell. Losses resulting from significant line sales are recognized in income when the asset meets the criteria for classification as held for sale whereas losses resulting from significant line abandonments are recognized in the statement of income when the asset ceases to be used. Gains are recognized in income when they are realized.

H. Depreciation

The cost of properties, including those under capital leases, net of asset impairment write-downs, is depreciated on a straight-line basis over their estimated useful lives as follows:

Asset class	Annual rate
Track and roadway	2%
Rolling stock	3%
Buildings	3%
Information technology	11%
Other	8%

The Company follows the group method of depreciation for railroad properties and, as such, conducts comprehensive depreciation studies on a periodic basis to assess the reasonableness of the lives of properties based upon current information and historical activities. Changes in estimated useful lives are accounted for prospectively. In 2007, the Company completed a depreciation study for all of its U.S. assets, for which there was no significant impact on depreciation expense. The Company is also conducting a depreciation study of its Canadian properties, plant and equipment, and expects to finalize this study by the first quarter of 2008.

Note 5 to the financial statements

5 Properties

In millions		*December 31, 2007*						*December 31, 2006*			
		Cost		Accumulated depreciation		Net		Cost		Accumulated depreciation		Net
Track and roadway [1]	$	22,020	$	6,433	$	15,587	$	22,579	$	6,445	$	16,134
Rolling stock		4,702		1,606		3,096		4,833		1,676		3,157
Buildings		1,105		498		607		1,251		609		642
Information technology		667		131		536		622		101		521
Other		829		242		587		1,226		627		599
	$	29,323	$	8,910	$	20,413	$	30,511	$	9,458	$	21,053
Capital leases included in properties												
Track and roadway [1]	$	457	$	38	$	419	$	450	$	25	$	425
Rolling stock		1,591		310		1,281		1,442		275		1,167
Buildings		119		2		117		38		3		35
Information technology		14		2		12		20		6		14
Other		211		63		148		188		41		147
	$	2,392	$	415	$	1,977	$	2,138	$	350	$	1,788

(1) *Includes the cost of land of $1,530 million and $1,746 million as at December 31, 2007 and 2006, respectively, of which $108 million was for right-of-way access and was recorded as a capital lease in both years.*

Canadian Pacific

From balance sheet

	2007	***2006***
Net properties (Note 12)	9,293.1	9,122.9

NET PROPERTIES

Fixed asset additions and major renewals are recorded at cost, including direct costs, directly attributable indirect costs and attributed carrying costs. The Company capitalizes development costs for major new computer systems, including the related variable indirect costs. In addition, CP capitalizes the cost of major overhauls and large refurbishments. When depreciable property is retired or otherwise disposed of in the normal course of business, the book value, less net salvage proceeds, is charged to accumulated depreciation. However, when removal costs exceed the salvage value on assets and the Company had no legal obligation to remove, the net removal cost is charged to income in the period in which the asset is removed and is not charged to accumulated depreciation. When there is a legal obligation associated with the retirement of property, plant and equipment, a liability is initially recognized at its fair value and a corresponding asset retirement cost is added to the gross book value of the related asset and amortized to expense over the estimated term to retirement. The Company reviews the carrying amounts of its properties whenever changes in circumstances indicate that such carrying amounts may not be recoverable based on future undiscounted cash flows. When such properties are determined to be impaired, recorded asset values are revised to the fair value and an impairment loss is recognized.

Depreciation is calculated on the straight-line basis at rates based on the estimated service life, taking into consideration the projected annual usage of depreciable property, except for rail and other track material in the U.S., which is based directly on usage. Usage is based on volumes of traffic.

Assets to be disposed of are included in "Other assets and deferred charges" on the Consolidated Balance Sheet. They are reported at the lower of the carrying amount and fair value, less costs to sell, and are no longer depreciated.

Equipment under capital lease is included in properties and depreciated over the period of expected use.

12. Net properties

(in millions of Canadian dollars)	Cost	Accumulated depreciation	Net book value
2007			
Track and roadway	**$ 8,828.0**	**$ 2,852.1**	**$ 5,975.9**
Buildings	**342.4**	**136.0**	**206.4**
Rolling stock	**3,593.7**	**1,485.4**	**2,108.3**
Other	**1,632.9**	**630.4**	**1,002.5**
Total net properties	**$ 14,397.0**	**$ 5,103.9**	**$ 9,293.1**
2006			
Track and roadway	$ 8,615.1	$ 2,770.5	$ 5,844.6
Buildings	344.8	154.1	190.7
Rolling stock	3,548.3	1,450.9	2,097.4
Other	1,625.6	635.4	990.2
Total net properties	$ 14,133.8	$ 5,010.9	$ 9,122.9

At December 31, 2007, software development costs of $612.5 million (2006 – $609.8 million) and accumulated depreciation of $239.1 million (2006 – $239.8 million) were included in the category "Other". Additions during 2007 were $48.8 million (2006 – $37.6 million; 2005 – $39.6 million) and depreciation expense was $50.5 million (2006 – $53.2 million; 2005 – $52.3 million).

At December 31, 2007, net properties included $503.4 million (2006 – $522.5 million) of assets held under capital lease at cost and related accumulated depreciation of $127.5 million (2006 – $112.4 million).

During 2007, capital assets were acquired under the Company's capital program at an aggregate cost of $908.5 million (2006 – $818.6 million; 2005 – $906.0 million), $12.1 million of which were acquired by means of capital leases (2006 – $21.6 million; 2005 – $0.6 million), and $4.6 million of which were acquired by means of a non-monetary transaction. Cash payments related to capital purchases were $893.2 million in 2007 (2006 – $793.7 million; 2005 – $884.4 million). At December 31, 2007, $2.1 million (2006 – $3.5 million; 2005 – $9.4 million) remained in accounts payable related to the above purchases.

Case 2

Locate the current financial statements of a company that owns intangible assets[1], and supply the following information. (Information has been supplied for Pfizer, as an example (http://www.pfizer.com/investors/financial_reports/financial_report_2007.jsp.)

Note: most large-cap companies engaged in manufacturing industrial or consumer products will have intangible assets of some sort. You can speed up your search by using a stock filter such as that found at www.globeinvestor.com.

Set the filter as follows:
 Industry = industrial products or consumer products
 Security = common
 Market Capitalization = 5,000 MM (minimum)

Example:

Item	Answer
Name of Company	Pfizer Inc.
Date of financial statements	December 31, 2007
Amount of intangible assets shown on balance sheet	Goodwill - $21, 382 MM Identifiable Intangible Assets less accumulated amortization - $20, 498 MM
Total assets	$115, 268 MM
Intangible assets expressed as a percent of total assets	(21,382 + 20,498)/115, 268 = 36%
Where is there further information about intangibles found on the financial statements?	Note 13
What types of intangible assets does the company own?	Goodwill Developed technology rights Brands License agreements Trademarks Other
Amount of amortization expense for intangibles for the year	$3,128 (from income statement)
Amortization expense as percent of profit (continuing operations) before taxes	amortization/(profit + amortization) = 3,128/(3, 128 ÷ 9,278) = 25%
Over what period are intangibles written off? State the source	Significant accounting policies – K Identifiable Intangible Assets are written off over their estimated useful life.
Was there any impairment of goodwill or intangibles? State the source	Yes – as per cash flow statement and note 13.

1 For Canadian company financial statements go to www.sedar.com; for U.S. companies go to http://www.sec.gov/edgar.shtml

Critical Thinking Exercise 1

a) Capital assets can constitute a significant portion of total assets. What specific criteria do you suggest for classifying an amount as a capital asset (i.e. cost, life, use)? Support your answer.

b) The calculation of depreciation may be performed using different methods. All methods are allowed under GAAP. Do you think that this is reasonable? Support your answer.

c) Which one method do you think is best for calculating depreciation? Support your answer.

d) Which one method is best for recording partial-year depreciation? Support your answer.

Critical Thinking Exercise 2

Since intangible assets have no physical existence, they cannot be seen. Stockholders may question showing an amount on the balance sheet for an "invisible" asset. Companies have staff with many years of experience who would be difficult to replace, and are therefore deemed valuable. However, the value of such staff is not reflected in the financial statements. Discuss.

Chapter 11

CURRENT LIABILITIES AND PAYROLL ACCOUNTING

Assessment Questions

Question 1

What are liabilities?

Question 2

Name the two classes of liabilities.

Question 3

How are current liabilities presented on the balance sheet?

Question 4

Define known (determinable) liabilities.

Question 5

Provide three examples of determinable (known) liabilities.

Question 6

Provide three examples of estimated or contingent (unknown) liabilities.

Question 7

Define accrued expenses.

Question 8

What is the normal source of funds used to pay current liabilities?

Question 9

How should the purchase of capital assets be financed?

Question 10

List the items you expect to find on a note payable.

Application Questions

Question 1

A company has repairs completed on the heating system. The service man hands the accountant an invoice for $1,000, due in one month. Write the journal entry to record this transaction.

DATE	DESCRIPTION	DR	CR

Question 2

A company uses substantial amounts of utilities (hydro and water) with an average cost of $6,000 per month. They receive and pay the actual bill on the 15th of each month. In January 2011, the company received their bill in the amount of $6,207 for the period December 15 to January 15. The bill was paid right away. Assume the company prepares monthly financial statements.

Required:

a) Give the journal entry to record the estimate of utilities expense for the period Dec. 16 – 31, 2010.

b) Record the journal entry required for payment of the bill on January 15, 2011.

DATE	DESCRIPTION	DR	CR

Question 3

Cervera Company borrowed $100,000 from the local branch. The loan is payable in equal installments over five years.

Required:

Write the journal entry to record the loan. Properly allocate the loan between current and long-term loan payable.

DATE	DESCRIPTION	DR	CR

Question 4

NOTE PAYABLE

For the Value Received, the undersigned promises to pay to the order of

U. Paymee the sum of

***** $5,000 and 00/100 Dollars *********************** ($5,000.00)

with annual interest of 7% on any unpaid balance. This note shall mature and be payable, along with accrued interest on:

July 31, 2011

February 1, 2011 | A. Notemaker

Issue Date | Maker Signature

Answer the following questions about the note shown above.

a) who is the lender?

b) who is the borrower?

c) when is payment due?

d) when was the note issued?

e) when is interest payable?

f) what amount must the borrower pay to the lender?

Question 5

On May 1, 2010, ACME Bank agreed to lend Mirza Enterprises $100,000. To that effect, Mirza signed a $100,000, 10-month, 12% note. Mirza Enterprises has a year-end of December 31.

Required:
Prepare the journal entry for Mirza Enterprises:

a) On the date the note was signed

b) At year-end

c) On March 1, 2011 when the note is repaid

DATE	DESCRIPTION	DR	CR

Question 6

On June 15, 2010, Actor Surplus agreed to lend Wei Hong Enterprises $250,000. To that effect, Wei signed a $250,000, 8-month, 10% note. Wei Hong Enterprises has a year-end of November 30.

Required:
Prepare the journal entry for Wei Hong Enterprises:

a) On the date the note was signed

b) At year-end

c) On February 16, 2011 when the note is repaid

DATE	DESCRIPTION	DR	CR

Question 7

Darren Spoon from Company ABC signed a 7% half-year note payable for $100,000 on November 1, 2010. The note is due with interest on May 1, 2011. Company ABC has a year-end of Dec 31.

Required:

a) journal entry recording receipt of cash

b) journal entry accruing interest at the year-end

c) ultimate payment of the note in the new year

DATE	DESCRIPTION	DR	CR

Question 8

Using the data in the following table (from the financial records of Nateghi Inc.), determine the salaries expense. Note that employer deductions have not yet been accrued for.

ACCOUNT NAME	DR	CR
Employees' Federal Income Tax Payable		1,250
Employees' State Income Tax Payable		750
Social Security Payable		800
Medicare/Medicaid Payable		300
Retirement Savings Payable		900
Charitable Donations Payable		250
Salaries and Wages Payable		12,380

Question 9

Part 1

On May 31, Saleem Enterprises had gross pay for employees of $42,500. Withholdings for employees are $2,635 for social security tax, $616 for Medicare tax, $1,570 for state income taxes, $7,060 for federal income taxes, and $1,700 for the retirement savings plan. Record the entry for wage expense on May 31.

Part 2

Using the data from Part 1 and assuming Saleem Enterprises contributes the same amount towards the employee retirement savings plan and will pay $561 to the Workers' Compensation board, prepare the journal entry for the employer's taxes and benefit costs.

Part 3

What is the total amount of cash that Saleem Enterprises will pay? How much will Saleem Enterprises pay for every $1.00 earned by employees?

Part 1

DATE	DESCRIPTION	DR	CR

Part 2

DATE	DESCRIPTION	DR	CR

Part 3

____

____

____

Question 10

Part 1

On September 30, Morales Inc. had gross pay for employees of $37,000. Withholdings for employees are $2,294 for social security tax, $536 for Medicare tax, $1,367 for state income taxes, $6,146 for federal income taxes, $1,300 for the retirement savings plan and $400 for charitable donations. Record the entry for wage expense on September 30.

Part 2

Using the data from Part 1 and assuming Morales Inc. does not contribute towards the employee retirement savings plan and will pay $425 to the Workers' Compensation board, prepare the journal entry for the employer's taxes and benefit costs.

Part 3

What is the total amount of cash that Morales Inc. will pay? How much will Morales Inc. pay for every $1.00 earned by employees?

Part 1

DATE	DESCRIPTION	DR	CR

Part 2

DATE	DESCRIPTION	DR	CR

Part 3

Question 11

The local transit company, in co-operation with local colleges and universities sells transit passes for the semester for $200 each. The passes are only sold prior to the start of the semester, and for the fall semester are good from September 1 to December 31. The transit company sold 1,000 passes on August 1.

Required:
Write the entry for:

a) The sale of the passes
b) The entry to be recorded on September 30.

DATE	DESCRIPTION	DR	CR

Question 12

Erik Tilly is starting a new business with some other investors. In addition, he is loaning the company $200,000 at a nominal rate of interest of 2% per annum and due in one year. Record the journal entry the new business has to make regarding the stockholder loan.

DATE	DESCRIPTION	DR	CR

Question 13

Lee-Yau Enterprises sells heavy-duty lawnmower equipment. Today, they sold a lawnmower (on account) for $45,000 which included a 4-year unlimited warranty. The corporation's accountant estimates that an amount of $3,000 will be paid out in warranty obligations. The cost of goods sold is $17,000. Assume Lee-Yau uses a perpetual inventory system. First, prepare the journal entry to record the sale and then prepare the entry to record the warranty.

DATE	DESCRIPTION	DR	CR

Question 14

Refer to the Question 13 above. Suppose Lee-Yau is required to repair the lawnmower sold (there is a faulty wire) and Lee-Yau spends $500 in cash remedying the problem. Record the journal entry for this transaction.

DATE	DESCRIPTION	DR	CR

Question 15

Los Amigos Manufacturing Ltd. builds and sells cars. They recently sold 150 cars for $30,000 each. The cost to build each car is $7,000. Los Amigos does not sell warranties with the purchase of the car; however, the customer has the option to purchase the warranty separately. Los Amigos sold a 4-year warranty for each car sold. Each warranty costs $2,000. Prepare the journal entries for the sale of the cars and warranties. Assume the cars were purchased on account and that the warranties were paid for in cash. Los Amigos uses a perpetual inventory system.

DATE	DESCRIPTION	DR	CR

Question 16

Refer to Question 15 above. Record the journal entry related to unearned warranty revenue at the end of 1 year from date of purchase of the cars.

DATE	DESCRIPTION	DR	CR

Question 17

Shown below is a partial balance sheet for a manufacturer.

	As at March 1, 2008	As at March 3, 2007
Assets		
Current		
Cash and cash equivalents (note 4)	1,184,398	677,144
Short-term investments (note 4)	420,709	310,082
Accounts receivables	1,249,381	612,811
Inventory (note 5)	396,267	255,907
Other current assets (note 18)	226,599	63,321
	3,477,354	1,919,265
Long-term investments (note 4)	738,889	425,652
Capital assets (note 6)	705,955	487,579
Intangible assets (note 7)	469,988	138,182
Goodwill (note 8)	119,001	118,271
	5,511,187	3,088,949
Liabilities		
Current		
Accounts Payable	271,076	130,270
Accrued Liabilities (notes 13 and 17(c))	690,442	287,629
Income taxes payable (note 9)	475,328	99,958
Deferred revenue	37,236	28,447
Current portion of long-term debt (note 10)	349	271
	1,474,431	546,575

Required:

a) Calculate the current ratio for 2008

b) Calculate the quick ratio for 2008

c) Comment on the current ratio and quick ratio

Case

- Locate the financial statements of a company with total assets greater than $1 billion.
- State the name of the company
- Note the date of the financial statements
- Locate the liabilities section
    - What is the amount of current liabilities?
    - What is the amount of long-term liabilities?
    - What is the amount of current assets?
    - What is the amount of owner's equity?
    - Calculate the ratio of total liabilities to owners' equity
    - Does the company have any stockholder loans?
- Calculate the current ratio
- Calculate the quick ratio
- Comment on the current and quick ratios
- Does the company have any contingencies?
- Review the notes to the financial statements. Summarize any notes related to liabilities

Critical Thinking Exercise

Contingent liabilities arise when the payment of a liability depends on uncertain future events, such as the result of a lawsuit.

Current accounting practice requires that when a contingent liability is likely, and the amount can be reasonably estimated, the amount must be accrued on the statement of financial position.

Is this practice reasonable, (in light of the fact that the liability is not definite), and only estimates are used? Does this practice mislead owners regarding the actual state of affairs surrounding liabilities? Discuss.

Notes

Chapter 12

LONG-TERM LIABILITIES

Assessment Questions

Question 1

Name the typical forms of long-term debt.

Question 2

What is a bond?

Question 3

An investor pays $83,333 for a bond, but will receive $100,000 when the bond matures. Has the investor bought the bond at a discount or at a premium?

Question 4

Bonds can be issued at different prices relative to their face value. Name the three types of bonds relative to face value.

Question 5

When would a bond be issued at a discount? At a premium?

Question 6

A $100,000 bond is issued for $110,000. Is the current market interest rate for bonds above or below the rate stated in the bond contract?

Question 7

What amount remains in the discount on bond amortized account or premium on bonds account related to a bond on the maturity date of the bond?

Question 8

What is generally considered the maximum acceptable debt-to-total-assets ratio? Why?

Question 9

Funds raised from long-term debt are used for what kind of investments?

Question 10

What is the difference between bonds and stocks?

____

____

____

____

____

____

____

Application Questions

Question 1

A company issued $500,000 of bonds at par. Write the journal entry to record the transaction.

DATE	DESCRIPTION	DR	CR

Question 2

A company issued $500,000 of bonds at a discount of 5%. Write the journal entry to record the transaction.

DATE	DESCRIPTION	DR	CR

Question 3

A company issued $500,000 of bonds at a premium of 1%. Write the journal entry to record the transaction.

DATE	DESCRIPTION	DR	CR

Question 4

A company is issuing $300,000 worth of 5-year bonds, bearing an interest rate of 4%. Assume that the current, market rate of interest is 5%.

a) Will the bond be issued at a discount or at a premium?

b) Calculate the value of the resulting discount or premium.

c) Record the journal entry to reflect the sale of bonds and the appropriate discount or premium.

Note that the present value factor for the principal is 0.784 (5%, 5-years) and that the present value factor for the recurring interest payments is 4.329 (5%, 5-years).

c)

DATE	DESCRIPTION	DR	CR

Question 5

Refer to question 4. Assuming interest is paid annually; write the journal entry to record payment of interest.

DATE	DESCRIPTION	DR	CR

Question 6

Shown below is a segment of the financial statements of a large company.

	As at	
	March 1, 2008	**March 1, 2009**
Assets		
Current		
Cash and Cash Equivalents (note 4)	**1,184,398**	677,144
Short-Term Investments (note 4)	**420,709**	310,082
Accounts Receivables	**1,174,692**	572,637
Other Receivables	**74,689**	40,174
Inventory (note 5)	**396,267**	255,907
Other Current Assets (note 18)	226,599	63,321
	3,477,354	1,919,265
Long-Term Investments (note 4)	**738,889**	425,652
Capital Assets (note 6)	**705,955**	487,579
Intangible Assets (note 7)	**469,988**	138,182
Goodwill (note 8)	**119,001**	118,271
	5,511,187	3,088,949
Liabilities		
Current		
Accounts Payable	**271,076**	130,270
Accrued Liabilities (notes 13 and 17 (c))	**690,442**	287,629
Income Taxes Payable (note 9)	**475,328**	99,958
Deferred Revenue	**37,236**	28,447
Current Portion of Long-Term Debt (note 10)	349	271
	1,474,431	546,575
Long-Term Debt (note 10)	**72,317**	58,874
Income Tax Payable	30,873	–
	1,577,621	605,449
Stockholder's Equity		
Contributed Capital (note 11)		
Authorized - unlimited number of non-voting, cumulative, redeemable, retractable preferred stocks; unlimited number of voting common stocks issued - 562,652,451 voting common stocks (March 1, 2008 - 557,613,432)	**2,169,856**	2,099,696
Retained Earnings	**1,653,094**	359,227
Paid-In Capital	**80,333**	36,093
Accumulated Other Comprehensive Income (loss) (note 16)	30,283	(11,516)
	3,933,566	2,483,500
	5,511,187	3,088,949

Calculate the debt-to-total assets ratio. Comment on the ratio. The formula for this ratio is:

$$\text{Debt to Total Assets Ratio} = \frac{\text{Total Liabilities}}{\text{Total Assets}}$$

____

____

____

____

Question 7

On April 30, year 1, a company issued $600,000 worth of 4% bonds. The term of the bonds is 10 years, with interest payable semi-annually. The year-end of the company is November 30. Record the journal entries related to interest for year 1, and year 2. Note that interest must be accrued at the end of each year.

DATE	DESCRIPTION	DR	CR

Question 8

Sam's Construction is a construction company (with a December 31 year-end) that is planning to expand its facilities by constructing a new building, and acquiring new equipment. In order to complete this project, the company has decided to issue $100,000 worth of 10-year bonds at 5% on March 1, 2010. The interest payment is made semi-annually on September 1 and March 1. Just as the company completes all the necessary contracts, and is ready to issue the bonds, the market rate increases to 6%, resulting in a price of $92,640 for these bonds.

Note: The premium/discount is amortized using the straight-line method.

a) Are these bonds issued at a discount or at a premium? Prepare the journal entry for the issuance of bonds on March 1, 2010.

b) Prepare the journal entry for the first payment of interest on September 1, 2010

c) Prepare the adjusting entry on December 31, 2010

a)

____

____

DATE	DESCRIPTION	DR	CR

b)

DATE	DESCRIPTION	DR	CR

c)

DATE	DESCRIPTION	DR	CR

Question 9

Burroughs Corporation (with a December 31 year-end) issued $450,000, 9.5% bonds due in 8 years on May 1, 2010. Interest is paid semi-annually on November 1 and May 1 of each year. On the issuance date, the market rate of interest was 8.5%, resulting in a price of $475,000 for these bonds.

Note: The premium/discount is amortized using the straight-line method.

a) Is this bond issued at a discount or at a premium? Prepare the journal entry on May 1, 2010, to issue the bonds.

b) Prepare the journal entry on November 1, 2010, to record the first interest payment and the amortization of the premium/discount.

c) Prepare the adjusting entry on December 31, 2010.

d) Show the balance sheet presentation of Bonds Payable and related accounts as at December 31, 2010.

a)

____

____

____

DATE	DESCRIPTION	DR	CR

b)

DATE	DESCRIPTION	DR	CR

c)

DATE	DESCRIPTION	DR	CR

d)

Question 10

Mustafa has recently graduated from an Aerospace Engineering program and is training to become an astronaut. Part of the training program includes a basic course in accounting and finance (it is important for astronauts to be well-rounded). Mustafa is posed with the following question on his exam:

MT Biotech has issued $3,500,000, 5% callable bonds due in 12 years. At the time of issue the market interest rate is 6% (interest is due annually). Calculate the discount at which the bonds were issued.

The following present value factors may be of use to you:

Single:

0.557 (5%, 12 years)

0.497 (6%, 12 years)

Annuity:

8.863 (5%, 12 years)

8.384 (6%, 12 years)

Unfortunately, Mustafa spent the previous day in the centrifuge (G-force training) and, as a result, he is finding it difficult to concentrate. Please help Mustafa solve this problem.

Case

Research and describe the role of credit rating agencies in the bond market.
Name three major credit rating agencies.
Describe and list the major categories of credit ratings for these agencies.

Critical Thinking Exercise

Companies can choose to record interest expense on bonds using the straight-line method, or by using a method that incorporates the time value of money. Which method do you recommend that a company use? Support your answer.

Chapter 13

PARTNERSHIPS

Assessment Questions

Question 1

Define a partnership.

Question 2

Compare and contrast characteristics of proprietorships and partnerships.

Characteristic	Proprietorship	Partnership

Question 3

List the different ways in which partnership earnings may be divided.

Question 4

What are the advantages of organizing a business as a partnership over a proprietorship?

Question 5

How is the division of partnership earnings decided?

Question 6

What methods may partners choose to pay themselves, other than straight division of profits?

Question 7

Explain the closing of the income summary account for partnerships.

Question 8

During the year, partners may withdraw cash or other assets. What account is used to accumulate these withdrawals?

Question 9

What happens to partners' drawings at year end?

Application Questions

Question 1

Chandra Heesch and Allie Owenby have decided to form a partnership on January 1, 2011. Each partner has agreed to contribute $10,000. Write the journal entry to record the beginning of the partnership.

DATE	DESCRIPTION	DR	CR

Question 2

Ted Coverdale and Julio Kadlec are setting up a new partnership on March 10, 2011. Ted will contribute a warehouse and land worth a combined $1,000,000. Market value of the warehouse is $300,000. Julio will contribute $1,000,000 in cash. Write the journal entry to record the contributions to the partnership.

DATE	DESCRIPTION	DR	CR

Question 3

Selena Hegarty, Cody Debruyn and Lenore Raap operate their business as a partnership. According to their partnership agreement, Selena and Lenore split 51% of the profits equally. The remainder of the profits goes to Cody. Record the entry for the division of profits of $100,000 on December 31, 2011. Assume that revenues and expenses have already been closed to the income summary account.

DATE	DESCRIPTION	DR	CR

Question 4

Mallory Longshore, Lakisha Laffey and Avis Hemsley set up a partnership at the beginning of 2011. Mallory contributed $10,000 in cash. Lakisha contributed a van worth $20,000. Avis contributed equipment worth $15,000. The partnership made $9,000 net income for the year. According to the partnership agreement, profits are divided in the ratio of their initial contributions. Record the entry for the division of the profits on December 31, 2011. Assume that revenues and expenses have already been closed to the income summary account.

DATE	DESCRIPTION	DR	CR

Question 5

Refer to question 4. Assume that the partnership recorded a loss of $4,500. Record the entry for the division of the loss. Assume that revenues and expenses have already been closed to the income summary account.

DATE	DESCRIPTION	DR	CR

Question 6

Tanisha Vanscyoc and Kurt Vicini operate a partnership that produces custom-made furniture. On April 12, Tanisha withdrew $50,000 in cash. On April 15, Kurt removed a sofa and chairs worth $30,000 for use in his own home. Write the journal entry to record these transactions.

DATE	DESCRIPTION	DR	CR

Question 7

Refer to question 6 above. Write the journal entry to close the Drawings accounts on December 31.

DATE	DESCRIPTION	DR	CR

Question 8

Noemi Loop, Lilia Hopkin and Guy Scoggin perform in a band operating as a partnership. According to the partnership agreement, Noemi receives a salary of $22,000, Lilia receives a salary of $30,000, and Guy a salary of $28,000. They are also to receive nominal interest of 5% on the capital at the end of the preceding year (Noemi - $1,000, Lilia - $10,000, Guy - $20,000). The remainder is divided equally. During the year partners withdrew $22,000 each as an advance to their share of partnership earnings. The band made $100,000 after paying all other expenses.

Required:

Prepare a table showing changes in the partners' capital during the year.

	Total	Loop	Hopkin	Scoggin

Question 9

Refer to question 8. Assume that the net income remaining is distributed on the ratio of the opening balance of capital. Prepare the schedule showing the changes in capital.

	Total	Loop	Hopkin	Scoggin

Question 10

Refer to question 9. Prepare the journal entry to recording the distribution of net income and close the drawings accounts on December 31. Assume that revenues and expenses have already been closed to the income summary account.

DATE	DESCRIPTION	DR	CR

Case

A partnership has sales of $500,000 and expenses of $400,000 before payment of partners' salaries, interest on capital, and charges for equipment.

There are two partners who own the business. Each partner will receive earnings based on four factors. Each partner will receive a salary of $40,000. Each partner will receive interest on capital contributions which amounts to $2,000 for Partner A, and $1,000 for Partner B. Partner B puts equipment into the business and receives $2,000 "rent" on the equipment each year. Remaining profits are divided equally. The opening balances of capital were, $200,000 for Partner A and $100,000 for Partner B .

During the year, the partners withdrew $30,000 as advances on their yearly salary.

Required:

a) Calculate the net income of the partnership.

b) Show the calculation of the share of income to be distributed to each partner.

c) Prepare journal entries to record the distribution of income, drawings, and closing entries.

d) Explain why salaries, interest and rental of equipment are not included in the closing entries.

e) Prepare the equity section of the statement of financial position.

a)

____

____

____

____

____

b)

	Total	**Partner A**	**Partner B**

c)

DATE	DESCRIPTION	DR	CR

d)

e)

A & B Partnership Statement of Partners' Equity As at dd/mm/yy			
	Partner A	Partner B	Total

Critical Thinking Exercise

Sometimes a person simply wants to invest in a business as an owner, rather than actively participate in the business. This is simple when the business is organized as a corporation. By definition, a proprietorship has only one owner. If the investor participates in a partnership, the investor assumes unlimited liability for the partnership.

Is it wise to invest in a partnership if one does not want to actively participate in the partnership?

Are there any steps an investor could take to limit their liability? Discuss.

Chapter 14

CORPORATIONS: CONTRIBUTED CAPITAL AND DIVIDENDS

Assessment Questions

Question 1

List the advantages and disadvantages of the corporate form of ownership.

Question 2

Which portion of the equity section of a set of corporate financial statements relates to money invested by the owners? Relates to accumulated earnings?

Question 3

You are preparing the financial statements for a corporation. You must disclose the number of stock authorized. Where would you find the number of shares authorized?

Question 4

What is meant by "outstanding shares"?

Question 5

Define "retained earnings".

Question 6

What may stock be issued for?

Question 7

What is the main difference between common and preferred stock?

Question 8

List the usual characteristics of common stock.

Question 9

List the usual characteristics of preferred stock.

Question 10

List and describe the three important dates associated with accounting for dividends.

Question 11

Who decides the amount of a dividend to be paid to stockholders? Discuss.

Application Questions

Question 1

Earnestine, Kepplinger & Co. issued 10,000 shares of common stock for $100,000. Write the journal entry to record the transaction.

DATE	DESCRIPTION	DR	CR

Question 2

Refer to Question 1. In addition to stock issued for cash, Earnestine, Kepplinger & Co. issued an additional 10,000 shares of common stock in exchange for land and a building. The land was valued at $60,000 and the building valued at $50,000. Record the transaction.

DATE	DESCRIPTION	DR	CR

Question 3

The lawyer that handled the issue of stocks discussed in questions 1 and 2 above has sent a bill for $5,000. The lawyer has agreed to accept 500 shares of common stock instead of cash. Record the transaction.

DATE	DESCRIPTION	DR	CR

Question 4

Neva Gillikin Limited had revenues of $5,000,000 and expenses of $4,500,000. Prepare the journal entries to close the accounts for the year.

DATE	DESCRIPTION	DR	CR

Question 5

Liang Inc. is authorized to issue an unlimited number of $8 par value common stock. Suppose 3,000 of these stock are sold for $14 each. Record the entry to record the issuance.

DATE	DESCRIPTION	DR	CR

Question 6

On July 1st Jonus Enterprises declares a dividend of $5,000 to stockholders on record on July 4th. Record the journal entry associated with this transaction.

DATE	DESCRIPTION	DR	CR

Question 7

Using the facts from Question 6, record the journal entry when Jonus Enterprises pays out the dividend on August 15th.

DATE	DESCRIPTION	DR	CR

Question 8

On November 1st, 2010, Mistry Inc. declared $850,000 of dividends payable to stockholders on January 15, 2011. There are 220,000 shares of common stock and 30,000, $4, cumulative shares of preferred stock. No dividends have been declared since 2006. Calculate how much Mistry Inc. owes the preferred stockholders. Write the journal entries to record the declaration and subsequent payout of the dividends.

DATE	DESCRIPTION	DR	CR

Question 9

On December 1st, 2010, Fickle Feline Inc. (a distributor of cat products) declared $200,000 of dividends payable to stockholders on January 3, 2011. There are 20,000 shares of common stock and 10,000, $0.5, cumulative preferred stock. No dividends have been declared since 2007. Calculate how much Fickle Feline Inc. owes the preferred stockholders. Write the journal entries to record the declaration and subsequent payout of the dividends.

DATE	DESCRIPTION	DR	CR

Question 10

Bishop Lutz Hockey Paraphernalia Ltd has 50,000 shares of common stock issued. On January 1st, 2010, the organization declared a 25% stock dividend. Give the journal entries to record the declaration and distribution (on February 1st, 2010) of the dividend. The current market price per stock is $15.

DATE	DESCRIPTION	DR	CR

Question 11

Silang Vayman Ltd is a travel agency that specializes in tours to the Philippines and Russia. It has 75,000 shares of common stock issued. On March 15th, 2010, the organization declared a 45% stock dividend. Give the journal entries to record the declaration and distribution (on April 1st, 2010) of the dividend. The current market price per stock is $25.

DATE	DESCRIPTION	DR	CR

Question 12

Naidu Inc. (a record company) decided to buy back 2,000 common shares of its own stock at a price of $10 per share. Give the journal entries to record the purchase.

DATE	DESCRIPTION	DR	CR

Question 13

Given the following data for Khan Enterprises, determine total stockholders' equity.

Treasury stock, common (2,000 shares of stock at cost)	20,000
Contributed capital	
Common stock, $10 par value 1, 000,000 shares of stock authorized,	
40,000 shares of stock issued, 38,000 shares of stock outstanding	2,000,000
Retained earnings	375,000
Additional paid–in capital	105,000

Case

McIntosh Pharmaceutical develops and manufactures cancer related drugs. For the last 10 years they have been developing a unique chemical that has been shown to reduce the risk of breast cancer in middle-aged women. Unfortunately, just before going into mass production, scientists within McIntosh uncovered harmful side-effects of the drug and strongly recommended to management that mass production be delayed for another 5 years so as to better study the drug. McIntosh management contemplated their response and after three days, they announced this news to the public. Following the announcement, McIntosh stock price dropped 40%. During the three days of meetings, however, many managers decided to sell their stock in McIntosh.

Was their decision to sell stock ethically sound? Why is insider trading not tolerated?

Critical Thinking Exercise

John Maynard Nash, a budding economist, noticed that the market price of stock seemed to decline after the date of record of a cash dividend. Can you suggest why this might be the case?

Notes

Chapter 15

CORPORATIONS: THE FINANCIAL STATEMENTS

Assessment Questions

Question 1

How are income taxes recorded for accounting purposes (cash basis vs accrual basis)?

Question 2

Define accounting income and taxable income.

Question 3

What does "deferred income taxes" refer to?

Question 4

Define discontinued operations.

Question 5

Define an extraordinary item.

Question 6

Define comprehensive income.

Question 7

What information must a corporation disclose relative to income and retained earnings?

Question 8

Define and discuss book value per share.

Question 9

What ratio is used to assess debt relative to the amount of equity? Discuss.

Question 10

What ratio is used to determine what amount of a company's earnings is paid out in dividends?

Question 11

How do you calculate earnings per share?

Application Questions

Question 1

At year end, Shuster Home Decor Inc. (a small home furnishings retail store run by Terri) has accounting income (before income tax expense calculation) of $102,000. Write the journal entry to record the income tax expense. Assume the tax rate is 30%.

DATE	DESCRIPTION	DR	CR

Question 2

At year end, F'Brae Cheerleading Inc. (a medium sized distributor of cheerleading outfits) has accounting income of $210,000. Write the journal entry to record the income tax expense. Assume the tax rate is 30%.

DATE	DESCRIPTION	DR	CR

Question 3

CoreeMonTeeth Dental Inc. is a manufacturer of high quality dental equipment. In the current year it had accounting income of $300,000 which included $40,000 of warranty expenses. Per state income taxation law, however, the warranty expenses are not deductible until they are actually paid. Write the journal entry to record income tax payable. Assume the tax rate is 30%.

DATE	DESCRIPTION	DR	CR

Question 4

Green Light Emissions Everyday (otherwise known as GLEE Inc.) has sales of $400,000 and expenses of $120,000 (before calculation of income tax expense). Prepare the income statement for GLEE taking into account income tax expense. Assume a tax rate of 30%.

GLEE Inc. **Income Statement** **For the year ending December 31, 20x2**		

Question 5

Born off the coast of Mykonos, Gregory displayed an aptitude for singing at a very early age. In high school, he joined a musical club that participated in numerous singing competitions. His stage name was "Gleek the Greek". Gregory decided that one day he would like to start his own singing school and is now taking an accounting course to help him become financially literate. He is posed with the following question on his test. Help him solve this question.

"Nacho Libray Inc. has income from continuing operations of $200,000. Their total expenses amounted to $100,000 and, of that, $50,000 pertained to income tax expense. Calculate the income tax rate used."

____

____

____

Question 6

The bookkeeper for GIFT Inc. noticed that she made an error when recording a $44,000 expenditure in the prior fiscal year. She booked the amount to the Repairs and Maintenance expense account instead of posting to the Equipment account. Write the journal entry that should be recorded to correct the Equipment account. Assume the tax rate is 30%.

DATE	DESCRIPTION	DR	CR

Question 7

An auditor noticed that TFK Inc. accidently recorded an insurance expenditure of $50,000 as an expense instead of properly recording it as a prepaid. The purchase was made on the last day of the fiscal period. Write the journal entry that should be recorded to correct the Prepaid Insurance account. Assume the tax rate is 30%.

DATE	DESCRIPTION	DR	CR

Question 8

Hello Company's balance sheet reported the following information related to the stockholders' equity section on December 31, 2010: Preferred stock, $3, cumulative, authorized 50,000, 11,000 shares issued for total proceeds of $770,000. Common stock, unlimited number authorized, 75,000 shares issued, $2,000,000. Retained earnings, $550,000. Assume the number of common and preferred shares remained constant throughout the year.

a) Prepare the stockholder's equity section of the balance sheet for Hello Company as at December 31, 2010.

b) Assuming there are two years dividends in arrears (including 2010), determine the book value per share of both common and preferred stock.

a)

Hello Company Partial Balance Sheet - Stockholders' Equity As at December 31, 2010	

b)

____

____

____

Question 9

Shown below are sections of the financial statements of Research in Motion. Calculate book value per share for 2008.

Stockholder's Equity	
Contributed Capital	
Authorized – unlimited number of non-voting, cumulative, redeemable, retractable preferred stock; unlimited number of non-voting, redeemable, retractable Class A common stock and an unlimited number of voting common stock issued – 562,652,461 voting common stock (March 3, 2007 – 557,613,432)	2,169,856
Retained Earnings	1,653,094
Paid-in Capital	80,333
Accumulated other comprehensive income (loss)	30,283
	3,933,566
Total Liabilities and Stockholder's Equity	5,511,187

Information regarding number of shares:

Balance as at March 3, 2007	557,613
Exercise of stock option	5,039
Balance at March 1, 2008	562,652

Question 10

Refer to question 9 above. The RIM income statement shows the following:

Net income	$1,293,897
Earnings per share	
Basic	$2.31
Diluted	$2.26

Calculate the earnings per share. Your calculation of EPS may not agree with the numbers shown above. See the Critical Thinking Exercise at the end of this chapter for further discussion.

Question 11

Research in Motion's balance sheet shows total liabilities of $1,577,621. Refer to the equity section of the statements shown in Question 9 above, and calculate the debt-to-equity ratio. Note your comments on the ratio.

Question 12

Part of the financial statements of Toromont Industries is shown below:

Consolidated Statements of Retained Earnings Years Ended December 31, 2007 ($ thousands)	
Retained Earnings, beginning of year	$477,820
Net Earnings	122,280
Dividends	(31,061)
Retained Earnings, end of year	$539,039

Calculate the dividend payout ratio and discuss.

Question 13

The following information was taken from the accounting records of Cutler Inc. at December 31, 2010.

Line Item	Amount
Prior-year error – debit to Retained Earnings	15,000
Income tax expense on operating income from discontinued operations	19,600
Total dividends	67,000
Common stock, 75,000 shares issued	201,000
Sales revenue	605,000
Income tax expense on extraordinary gain	21,000
Interest expense	17,000
Extraordinary gain	60,000
Operating income, discontinued operations	56,000
Loss due to lawsuit	16,000
Sales Discounts	30,000
Income tax savings on sale of discontinued operations (sold at a loss)	(8,750)
General expenses	23,000
Income tax expense on continuing operations	73,150
Preferred stock, $7.00, 1,000 shares issued	60,000
Retained Earnings, January 1, 2010 (prior to adjustment)	135,000
Loss on sale of discontinued operations	25,000
Cost of goods sold	310,000

Required:

1. Prepare a multi-step income statement for the year ended December 31, 2010.
2. Prepare a statement of retained earnings for Cutler Inc. for the year ended December 31, 2010.
3. Calculated the EPS ratio.

Assume a tax rate of 35%. During the year, no new shares were issued or redeemed.

Part 1

Cutler Inc.
Income Statement
For the year ending December 31, 2010

Part 2

Cutler Inc.
Statement of Retained Earnings
For the year ending December 31, 2010

Part 3

____

____

____

Case

Obtain the current financial statements of a large capitalization company (i.e. > $5Billion), and answer the following questions.

a) Name of company	
b) Capitalization of the company	
c) Industry in which the company is engaged	
d) Contributed capital amount	
e) Retained earnings amount	
f) Total Liabilities	
g) Total stockholders' equity	
h) Debt-to-Equity Ratio	
i) Earnings per share (basic)	
j) Dividend per share	
k) Dividend payout ratio	
l) Book value per share (show calculation)	
m) Current market price per share (note the date)	

Critical Thinking

In this chapter, you have learned how to calculate book value per share, and earnings per share. Often, a corporation's annual report will report earnings per share and book value per share as calculated by the corporation. Rarely do the corporation's reported earnings per share or book value per share agree with a financial analyst's calculation of these numbers. Discuss why these two numbers may differ.

Chapter 16

THE CASH FLOW STATEMENT

Assessment Questions

Question 1

What information can be found on the cash flow statement?

Question 2

Is the amount of sales reported on the income statement equal to cash received? Explain.

Question 3

Is the amount reported as expenses on the income statement equal to cash paid out?

Question 4

Name the three sections shown on the cash flow statement.

Question 5

What items are included in each section of the cash flow statement?

Question 6

What effect do the following have on cash for the year?

- An increase in net income
- A decrease in receivables
- An increase in payables

Question 7

What effect do the following have on cash for the year?

- The purchase of long-term assets
- The payment of bank loan
- The payment of dividends

Question 8

Name five accounts, that when changed, will be disclosed in the operating section of the cash flow statement.

Question 9

State the effect (increase or decrease) of each of the following on cash:

1. profit for the year
2. depreciation
3. increase in prepaid expense
4. decrease in inventory
5. increase in accounts payable
6. sale of long-term assets
7. loan from a stockholder
8. loan from a bank
9. dividends

Question 10

Dreamlyma Inc possesses only tangible capital assets and records depreciation for all these assets in one Accumulated Depreciation account. If, at year end, Dreamlyma Inc. had Accumulated Depreciation of $30,000 in 2009 and Accumulated Depreciation of $45,000 in 2010, what was the depreciation expense on the income statement for the same period?

Question 11

At 2009 year-end, Lin-Z Inc. had retained earnings of $200,000. By 2010 year end it had retained earnings of $210,000. If net income for the 2010 fiscal year was $40,000, what amount of dividends was paid out in 2010?

Application Questions

Question 1

In which section of the cash flow statement would each of the following items be located?

1. Change in accounts payable
2. Change in inventory
3. Change in long-term loan
4. Change in other assets
5. Change in long-term assets
6. Change in prepaids
7. Change in receivables
8. Change in retained earnings (as a result of net income or net loss)
9. Change in contributed capital
10. Change in taxes payable

Change in Accounts Payable	
Change in Inventory	
Change in Long-Term Loan	
Change in Other Assets	
Change in Long-Term Assets	
Change in Prepaids	
Change in Receivables	
Change in Retained Earnings (as a result of net income or net loss)	
Change in Contributed Capital	
Change in Taxes Payable	

Question 2

Classify each of the following as either an increase or decrease in cash.

1. Net income
2. Increase in payables
3. Decrease in receivables
4. Purchase of long-term assets
5. Payment of bank loan

6. Increase in inventory
7. Payment of dividends
8. Increase in stockholder loans
9. Increase in prepaid expense

	Effect on Cash
Net Income	
Increase in payables	
Decrease in receivables	
Purchase of long-term assets	
Payment of bank loan	
Increase in inventory	
Payment of dividends	
Increase in stockholder loans	
Increase in prepaid expense	

Question 3

Classify each of the following as either an increase or decrease in cash.

1. Increase in accounts payable
2. Increase in inventory
3. Increase in long-term loan
4. Increase in other assets
5. Increase in prepaids
6. Increase in receivables
7. Increase in retained earnings (as a result of net income or net loss)
8. Increase in contributed capital
9. Increase in taxes payable

Increase in accounts payable	
Increase in inventory	
Increase in long-term loan	
Increase in other assets	
Increase in prepaids	
increase in receivables	
Increase in retained earnings	
increase in contributed capital	
Increase in taxes payable	

Question 4

Varnum Ltd. declared a stock dividend (Dr. Retained Earnings, Cr. Common Stock) of $50,000. How is the dividend reported on the cash flow statement?

____

____

____

Question 5

CCL Industries had net earnings of $147,915, including depreciation of $75,912. The balance sheet showed the following:

	2010	2009
Current Assets	391,023	424,897
Cash	96,602	125,000
Current Liabilities	244,966	322,996

Calculate the increase or decrease in cash from operations based on the information provided.

Question 6

A company reported the following:
Calculate the change and direction (increase, decrease) in cash from financing based on the information provided.

Opening Cash	$120,193
Increase in cash from operations	161,298
Increase in cash from investment	9,272
Closing Cash	$125,000

Question 7

Shown below is a sample of descriptions taken from an actual cash flow statement. Indicate the section to which the item belongs (operations, investing, financing).

Item	Section
Additions to Property, Plant and Equipment	
Depreciation and Amortization	
Dividends	
Gain on Sale of Property, Plant and Equipment	
Increase (decrease) in Bank Advances	
Issue of Stock	
Long-Term Investment Acquisition	
Proceeds from Disposal of Property, Plant and Equipment	
Proceeds on Issuance of Long-Term Debt	

Question 8

The following information was presented in the financial statements of Star Media Corp. Their year-end is December 31, 2010.

Star Media Corp. Income Statement For the year ended December 31, 2010	
Sales	$80,000
Cost of Goods Sold	50,000
Depreciation	6,000
Other Expenses	4,000
Net Income	$20,000

Star Media Corp. Comparative Balance Sheet As at December 31, 2010			
Assets	**2010**	**2009**	**Change**
Cash	$5,000	$4,000	$1,000
Accounts Receivable	5,000	4,000	1,000
Inventory	3,000	2,000	1,000
Prepaid Expenses	2,000	0	2,000
Equipment	105,000	100,000	5,000
Accumulated Depreciation	(36,000)	(30,000)	(6,000)
Total Assets	$84,000	$80,000	$4,000
Liabilities			
Accounts Payable	$8,000	$6,000	$2,000
Accrued Liabilities	1,000	2,000	(1,000)
Notes Payable	10,000	12,000	(2,000)
Total Liabilities	19,000	20,000	(1,000)
Stockholders' Equity			
Common Stock	22,000	20,000	2,000
Retained Earnings	43,000	40,000	3,000
Total Stockholders' Equity	65,000	60,000	5,000
Total Liabilities and Stockholders' Equity	$84,000	$80,000	$4,000

Additional information:

In addition to receiving cash from sales of their products, Star Media paid their suppliers and other expenses as they came due plus bought some new equipment, paid off some of the notes payable, issued new stock and paid out cash dividends. Assume accounts payable pertains solely to inventory and that operating expenses were paid in cash.

Required:

Using the above, you have been asked to prepare the Cash Flow Statement for Star Media Corp. for the year ending December 31, 2010 using the direct and the in-direct approach for the cash flows from operating activities.

	Inflow/(Outflow)	

	Inflow/(Outflow)	

Question 9

The following information was presented in the financial statements of Fisher Corporation for their year ended December 31, 2010.

Fisher Corporation Income Statement For the year ended December 31, 2010	
Sales	$130,600
Cost of Goods Sold	71,000
Depreciation	12,000
Other Expenses	22,000
Net Income	$25,600

Fisher Corporation Comparative Balance Sheet October 31, 2010			
Assets	**2010**	**2009**	**Change**
Cash	$59,000	$23,000	$36,000
Accounts Receivable	27,000	29,000	(2,000)
Inventory	30,000	36,000	(6,000)
Property and Equipment	111,000	96,000	15,000
Accumulated Depreciation	(36,000)	(24,000)	(12,000)
Total Assets	$191,000	$160,000	$31,000
Liabilities			
Accounts Payable	$25,000	$20,000	$5,000
Salaries Payable	800	3,000	(2,200)
Notes Payable	38,000	50,000	(12,000)
Total Liabilities	63,800	73,000	(9,200)
Stockholder's Equity			
Common Stock	80,000	58,000	22,000
Retained Earnings	47,200	29,000	18,200
Total Stockholders' Equity	127,200	87,000	40,200
Total Liabilities and Stockholders' Equity	$191,000	$160,000	$31,000

Additional information:

1. Bought equipment for cash, $15,000
2. Paid $12,000 on the long-term note
3. Issued new stock for $22,000
4. Declared and paid a $7,400 cash dividend.

Assume accounts payable pertains solely to inventory and that operating expenses were paid in cash.

Required:

Prepare the statement of cash flows for the year ended December 31, 2010 using the indirect method.

	Inflow/(Outflow)	

Question 10

The following information was presented in the financial statements of Comet Group Inc. for their year ended December 31, 2010.

Comet Group Inc. Income Statement For the year ended December 31, 2010	
Sales	882,600
Cost of Goods Sold	721,600
Depreciation	?
Other Operating Expenses	6,000
Interest Expense	4,000
Income Tax Expense	4,000
Net Income	?

Comet Group Inc. Comparative Balance Sheet December 31, 2010		
Assets	**2010**	**2009**
Cash	$11,800	$32,700
Accounts Receivable	84,200	88,000
Inventory	197,000	180,200
Prepaid Expenses	5,000	4,000
Equipment	245,000	200,000
Accumulated Depreciation	(43,200)	(12,600)
Land	81,000	18,500
Total Assets	$580,000	$510,800
Liabilities		
Accounts Payable	$21,600	$35,600
Interest Payable	17,600	13,000
Salaries Payable	14,400	3,000
Other Accrued Liabilities	36,000	38,000
Income-Tax Payable	15,000	8,000
Notes Payable	85,000	130,000
Total Liabilities	189,600	227,600
Stockholder's Equity		
Common Stock	283,000	244,000
Retained Earnings	108,200	39,200
Total Stockholders' Equity	391,200	283,200
Total Liabilities and Stockholders' Equity	$580,800	$510,800

Additional information:
Comet Group Inc. had no sales of plant and equipment or land, no new issuance of notes payable.
Assume accounts payable pertains solely to inventory, and that operating expenses were paid in cash. Also assume that the interest pertains to late payments to suppliers.

Required:

Prepare the cash flow statement using the indirect method. Show your calculations.

	Inflow/(Outflow)	

Question 11

The following information was presented in the financial statements of Lloyd's Lighting Ltd. for their year ended December 31, 2010.

Lloyd's Lighting Ltd. Comparative Balance Sheet December 31, 2010		
Assets		
Current Assets	**2010**	**2009**
Cash	$45,200	$14,000
Accounts Receivable	63,200	54,000
Interest Receivable	5,200	1,200
Inventory	107,200	115,000
Prepaid Expenses	5,000	3,200
Capital Assets		
Plant and Equipment, Rent	145,000	120,800
Accumulated Depreciation	(32,000)	(22,000)
Land	166,000	108,000
Total Assets	$504,800	$394,200
Liabilities		
Current Liabilities		
Accounts Payable	$62,800	$58,200
Interest Payable	8,800	9,200
Salaries Payable	6,200	14,000
Other Accrued Liabilities	27,400	31,200
Income Tax Payable	17,800	15,800
Long-Term Liabilities		
Notes Payable	150,000	190,000
Total Liabilities	273,000	318,400
Stockholder's Equity		
Common Stock	116,600	69,000
Retained Earnings	115,200	6,800
Total Stockholders' Equity	231,800	75,800
Total Liabilities & Stockholders' Equity	$504,800	$394,200

Lloyd's Lighting Ltd. Income Statement For the year ended December 31, 2010		
Sales Revenue		$520,000
Cost of Goods Sold		153,200
Gross Profit		366,800
Operating Expenses		
Salaries Expense	$55,600	
Depreciation Expense	10,000	
Other Operating Expenses	21,000	
Interest Expense	$23,200	109,800
Operating Income		257,000
Other Revenue and Expenses		
Interest Revenue		7,000
Income before Income Tax		264,000
Income Tax Expense		55,600
Net Income		$208,400

Additional information:
Assume there were no sales of plant and equipment or land and no issuance of new notes payable. Assume that accounts payable pertains to inventory purchases.

Required:

Prepare the cash flow statement using the indirect method.

	Inflow/(Outflow)	

Question 12

Using the following information from their accounting records, prepare the cash flow statement for Alvirina Corporation (year-end December 31, 2011) using the direct method.

Amortization Expense of	$12,000
Cash Sales of	314,000
Credit Sales of	500,000
Dividends received from investments in stock of	2,000
Warranty Expense of	5,000
Cash received issuing common stock of	10,000
Sale of capital assets for cash	20,000
Payments to suppliers of	15,000
Cost of Goods Sold of	212,000
Dividends paid of	23,000
Cash purchase of capital assets amounting to	150,000
Cash balance on January 1, 2011	165,000
Cash balance on December 31, 2011	$323,000

Question 13

Using the following information from their accounting records, prepare the cash flow statement for E-Game Corporation (year-end July 31, 2011) using the direct method.

Cash sales of	$278,000
Cash received from sale of investments,	34,000
Payments to employees (in cash) of	240,000
Cash received issuing common stock of	20,000
Sale of capital assets for cash	65,000
Interest received (in cash) on notes receivable of	19,000
Payments to suppliers of	7,000
Cost of Goods Sold of	112,000
Dividends paid of	100,000
Cash purchase of capital assets amounting to	50,000
Dividends received from investments in stock of	4,000
Cash balance on August 1, 2010	34,000
Cash balance on July 31, 2011	$57,000

Case

Shown below are the balance sheets for Dorel Industries for December 31, 2009 and 2010.

Required:

Prepare the statement of cash flow for 2010. Research any items you have not encountered before.

Dorel Industries Balance Sheet As at December 31, 2010		
Assets	**2010**	**2009**
Current Assets		
Cash	$22,513	$25,925
Accounts Receivable	286,924	294,731
Income Taxes Receivable	6,519	8,264
Inventory	322,332	326,540
Prepaid Expenses	10,538	9,652
Future Income Taxes	35,228	29,046
Total Current Assets	684,054	694,158
Long-Term Assets		
Property Plant and Equipment	333,772	312,213
Accumulated Depreciation	(193,410)	(170,211)
Net Book Value	140,362	142,002
Intangible Assets	276,383	261,986
Goodwill	525,235	501,336
Total Long-Term Assets	941,980	905,324
Other Assets	31,870	27,924
Total Assets	$1,657,904	$1,627,406
Liabilities		
Current Liabilities		
Bank Indebtedness	$5,836	$3,733
Accounts Payable	325,938	326,915
Income Taxes Payable	25,532	10,742
Balance of Sale Payable	--	605
Future Income Taxes	79,771	74,833
Current Portion of Long-Term Debt	62,906	7,832
Total Current Liabilities	499,983	424,660

Long-Term Liabilities		
Long-Term Debt	192,385	375,135
Pension Obligations	20,942	20,370
Other Long-Term Debt	6,848	7,719
Total Long-Term Liabilities	220,175	403,224
Total Liabilities	720,158	827,884
Stockholders' Equity		
Capital Stock	177,271	162,555
Contributed Surplus	11,623	6,061
Retained Earnings		
Opening Retained Earnings	567,020	478,155
Income for the Year	87,672	88,865
Dividends Paid	(12,711)	–
Closing Retained Earnings	641,981	567,020
Accumulated Other Comprehensive Income	106,871	63,886
Total Stockholder's Equity	937,746	799,522
Total Liabilities and Stockholder's Equity	$1,657,904	$1,627,406

	Inflow/(Outflow)	

Critical Thinking Exercise

The requirement that a statement of cash flow be included with other financial statements of a company is a recent requirement. Discuss the advantages and disadvantages of including the cash flow statement. Why do you think that various accounting bodies decided to include the statement of cash flows?

Notes

Chapter 17

FINANCIAL STATEMENT ANALYSIS

Assessment Questions

Question 1

What is the purpose of financial statement analysis?

Question 2

List the financial statement ratios related to the income statement that are covered in this course.

Question 3

Which financial ratio links the income statement and the balance sheet? Explain your answer.

Question 4

Which financial ratios indicate how well a company is managing its debt?

Question 5

Which financial ratios indicate how well a company is managing its assets?

Question 6

A company's debt to equity is 0.75:1, calculate the equity to debt ratio. What do these ratios indicate about the financial health of the company?

Question 7

Why are interest, tax, depreciation and amortization expenses ignored when calculating EBITDA?

Question 8

Why is it necessary to compare a company's calculated ratios with industry benchmarks?

Question 9

What is the possible result of a company having a poor debt to equity ratio?

Application Questions

Question 1

A company reported the following:

- Sales $1MM
- Cost of Sales $0.7MM
- Operating Expenses $0.4MM
- Income taxes $0.2MM

Calculate the gross profit margin. Differentiate gross profit margin and gross profit.

Question 2

Gross Profit increased from $0.3MM in period 1, to $0.4MM in period 2. Gross profit margin decreased from 30% in period 1, to 28% in period 2. Comment on whether or not the company's profitability improved or deteriorated in period 2.

Question 3

What factors can affect a company's gross profit margin?

Question 4

A company reported the following:

- Sales	$2.0MM
- Cost of Sales	0.7MM
- Operating Expenses	0.4MM
- Depreciation included in operating expenses	0.1MM
- Interest expense included in operating expenses	0.05MM
- Income taxes	40% of income before tax
- Owners' Equity (Average)	$20.0MM

Required: Calculate the EBITDA

Question 5

Use the information supplied in Question 4. Calculate the net profit margin.

Question 6

Use the information supplied in Question 4. Calculate the interest coverage ratio.

Question 7

Use the information supplied in Question 4. Calculate the return on equity. Banks are currently paying interest on deposits of 4% for money invested for 2 or more years. Comment on the ratio.

Question 8

A company reports current assets of $6,572, and current liabilities of $2,786. Calculate the current ratio.

Question 9

Refer to Question 8. If cash is $2,000, short-term investments are $3,000, long-term investments are $1,000 and net accounts receivable is $1,200, calculate the quick ratio.

Question 10

A company had a debt to equity ratio last year of 1.46. This year, the ratio is 2.0. Are things getting better or worse? Explain your answer.

Question 11

ABC Company sells on credit, with the balance payable in 30 days. The company's DSO ratio has changed from 60 days last year to 42 days this year. Are things getting better or worse? Explain the relationship between the sales terms and DSO.

Question 12

At the end of 2009, accounts receivable amounts to $210,000. At the beginning of the year it was $200,000. Net credit sales for the year amounted to $900,000 and net income was calculated to be $205,000.

Determine the days sales outstanding ratio and the accounts receivable turnover ratio.

Question 13

At the beginning of 2009, Acatela Corp. had inventory of $350,000. During the year, they purchased $220,000 worth of raw materials. From their income statement for fiscal 2009, cost of goods sold amounted to $500,000. Determine the inventory turnover ratio and the inventory days on hand ratio.

Question 14

The following information has been taken from the financial statements of Ivory Inc.

Ivory Inc.	
Current Assets, December 31, 2010	175,000
Total Assets, January 1, 2010	500,000
Total Assets, December 31, 2010	575,000
Current Liabilities, December 31, 2010	75,000
Total Liabilities, December 31, 2010	175,000
Stockholders' Equity, January 1, 2010	300,000
Stockholders' Equity, December 31, 2010	400,000
Net Sales	900,000
Depreciation	10,000
Interest Expense	20,000
Income Tax Expense	25,000
Net Income	40,000

1. Given the above data for Ivory Inc., calculate the following ratios for 2010 in the table below (round to two decimal places):

	Ratio	2009
a)	Current Ratio	3.5
b)	Interest Coverage Ratio	5.40
c)	Debt to Equity	25.00%
d)	Return on Assets	12.50%
e)	Return on Equity	20.20%
f)	Net Profit Margin	8.60%

2. Using 2009 as a comparison, discuss whether the company improved or deteriorated in its ability to (a) pay current liabilities as they come due, (b) meet its long-term debt obligations and (c) profitability. Be sure to make reference to specific ratios in your answers.

	Ratio	2010	2009
a)	Current Ratio = Current Assets/Current Liabilities		3.5:1
b)	Interest Coverage Ratio = EBITDA / Interest Expense		5.40:1
c)	Debt to Equity = Liabilities / Ending Equity		25.00%
d)	Return on Assets = Net Income / Average Total Assets		12.50%
e)	Return on Equity = Net Income / Average Stockholder's Equity		20.20%
f)	Net Profit Margin = Net Income / Sales		8.60%

a) ______________________________

____

____

____

b) ______________________________

____

____

____

c) ______________________________

____

____

____

Question 15

Perform a horizontal analysis for Groff Inc. Use 2007 as the base year and comment on the results.

Groff Inc.				
In Millions of Dollars				
	2010	2009	2008	2007
Revenue	500	400	300	200
Net Income	166	158	144	120

Groff Inc.				
In Millions of Dollars				

Question 16

Perform a vertical analysis (use Sales as the base) for Hiltonia Inc. Comment on the results. Note that figures are in millions of dollars.

	Hiltonia Inc.	
	2010	**2009**
Sales	210	250
COGS	150	200
Gross Profit	60	50
Selling Expenses	5	4
Wages	2	2
Rent	5	5
Total Expenses	12	11
Income before tax	48	39
Taxes (35%)	16.8	13.65
Net Income	31.2	25.35

	Hiltonia Inc.			
	2010	% of Sales	2009	% of Sales
Sales				
COGS				
Gross Profit				
Selling Expenses				
Wages				
Rent				
Total Expenses				
Income before tax				
Taxes (35%)				
Net Income				

Case

The following information is shown for Research in Motion for 2008 and 2007. Complete the following table. State the following: a) if the ratio has increased or decreased and b) whether this was a positive or negative change for the company.

Name of Company : Research in Motion		
	2008	**2007**
EBITDA Percentage to Sales	40.6%	44.4%
Gross Profit Margin	21.6%	20.8%
Interest Coverage Ratio	4.70 times	3.27 times
Return on Equity	32.9%	25.4%
Current Ratio	2.36	3.51
Quick Ratio	1.89	2.85
Debt to Equity Ratio	1:1	0.5:1
Days Sales Outstanding	71.37 days	68.87 days
Inventory Days on Hand	49.36 days	67.76 days

Name of Company : Research in Motion				
	2008	**2007**	**Increasing or Decreasing**	**Positive / Negative Impact**
EBITDA Percentage to Sales	40.6%	44.4%		
Gross Profit Margin	21.6%	20.8%		
Interest Coverage Ratio	4.70 times	3.27 times		
Return on Equity	32.9%	25.4%		
Current Ratio	2.36	3.51		
Quick Ratio	1.89	2.85		
Debt to Equity Ratio	1:1	0.5:1		
Days Sales Outstanding	71.37 days	68.87 days		
Inventory Days on Hand	49.36 days	67.76 days		

Critical Thinking Exercise

Financial statement analysis is performed on historical information. Since the past can't be changed, calculating financial ratios is of no use. What management and investors are really interested in is the future, specifically the future profitability of a company. Discuss.

Notes